P9-CMY-675

HODGES UNIVERSITY
LIBRARY - NAPLES

The Black Middle Class

The Black Middle Class

Social Mobility— and Vulnerability

Benjamin P. Bowser

LYNNE
RIENNER
PUBLISHERS

BOULDER
LONDON

Published in the United States of America in 2007 by
Lynne Rienner Publishers, Inc.
1800 30th Street, Boulder, Colorado 80301
www.rienner.com

and in the United Kingdom by
Lynne Rienner Publishers, Inc.
3 Henrietta Street, Covent Garden, London WC2E 8LU

© 2007 by Lynne Rienner Publishers, Inc. All rights reserved

Library of Congress Cataloging-in-Publication Data
Bowser, Benjamin P.
    The Black middle class : social mobility—and vulnerability / Benjamin P.
Bowser.
        p.   cm.
    Includes bibliographical references and index.
    ISBN-13: 978-1-58826-455-8 (hardcover : alk. paper)
    1. African Americans—Social conditions—1975–   2. African
Americans—Economic conditions.   3. Middle class—United States.   4. Social
classes—United States.   5. Social mobility—United States.   6. United
States—Social conditions—1980–   7. United States—Economic
conditions—1945–   8. United States—Race relations.   I. Title.
E185.86.B643 2006
305.5'508996073—dc22

                                                    2006015765

British Cataloguing in Publication Data
A Cataloguing in Publication record for this book
is available from the British Library.

Printed and bound in the United States of America

⊗   The paper used in this publication meets the requirements
     of the American National Standard for Permanence of
     Paper for Printed Library Materials Z39.48-1992.

    5   4   3   2   1

Contents

Tables and Figures

Tables

Figures

1

Introduction

Why should you read this book about the black middle class in the United States? An answer that you might least expect is self-interest. An objective of this book is to help you better understand the vulnerabilities of being middle class in the United States today. Underneath the anxieties that the white middle class has about affirmative action is an unarticulated concern that its privileges and economic circumstances are eroding relative to those of the black middle class. These anxieties exist largely because it is not clear who is middle class or what it takes to become and stay in the middle class. It is equally unclear what circumstances can lead to its decline and which of these conditions and circumstances are operating today.

Answering the unknowns about class will also lead to a clearer understanding of the continuing role of race and racism in the United States. The same fundamental issues are at the heart of both class- and race-based inequities. One door leads to the next. That is, important aspects of middle-class life in the United States cannot be fully understood or appreciated unless real race-based differences in social class are acknowledged and explored. The black middle-class experience is one of the best barometers of the changing fortune of the middle class writ large. Being middle class is itself a high-wire act, where actors rise and fall based on larger relationships between the wealthy and powerful and between the poor and powerless. This has been the case historically in the United States and continues to be so.

In the minds of many Americans, the emerging crisis of the middle class is not part of the black middle-class experience at all, leading to the belief that nothing can be learned about this crisis by looking at that black experience. This is so because most Americans, regardless of race, do not realize that the black middle class is an intrinsic part of the overall middle class in the United States. The omission of the black experience is evident in a sampling of books on middle-class crises published in the past decade (Glassman, 2000; Skocpol, 2000; Strobel, 1999; Sullivan, Warren, and Westbrook, 2000). Marginalizing blacks suggests either that issues about racial inequality and past differences have been completely addressed or that the continuing preoccupation with race is a problem only for black people. In reality, we are a long way from settling the issue of race in the United States. Studying the circumstances of black Americans and their responses to their situation is one of the best ways to understand the poorly articulated issues that everyone in the middle class is facing now or the hidden issues they will face in the near future.

The two worlds of blacks and whites have been distinct and unequal since the beginning of the republic, but they have never been separate. Figuratively, black Americans are the "the miner's canary" who is the first to die when toxic gas seeps into a mine (Guinier, 2005). When it comes to problems in US society and how it is governed, the problems and the outcome of governance will be most evident first among African Americans. The reason for this is that blacks have fewer resources to shield them from the impact of adverse government policies and business decisions, and their place in US society is heavily dependent upon the extent to which social justice overrides the presumption of white racial superiority.

What few Americans appreciate is that, apart from Native Americans, black Americans are second in tenure only to the original English settlers in terms of the length of time they have been in the United States. Yet, blacks invariably have been the people at the bottom of the social hierarchy (with Native Americans). Black survival is always in question and a miracle in each generation. And although it is true that what happens in White America impacts Black America, it is more important to know that what is hidden in White America is obvious and visible in Black America. The fundamental struggles that black Americans encounter and deal with in public are the same struggles that white Americans deal with in private or will soon face themselves if the problems are left unresolved. For example, in recent decades we have witnessed among blacks the emergence of drug abuse, declining quality of public education, rising divorce and separation rates, and mothers having children without the fathers being present. None of the issues underlying these problems has been resolved, so now they are becoming increasingly apparent among whites as well. W.E.B. Du Bois (Du Bois, 1903) was the first to point out this connection between blacks and whites and to examine the timing of when issues become apparent. This connection is still one of the most important and least understood realities about race in the US experience today.

Likewise, there are important aspects of being black and middle class in the United States that cannot be fully understood or appreciated by writing as if the black middle class is a world unto itself. Most of what you read about the black middle class portrays it as if it is isolated from the rest of society and without comparison. Such literature is long on description but short on explanation and comparison. The usual descriptions are about what people in the black middle class feel, think, and believe and about how they act (Barnes, 2000; Cose, 1993; Feagin and Sikes, 1994; Fulwood, 1996). Then there are critical assessments of what this class should be doing to address the plight of all blacks, as if those in the middle class have the power and circumstance to uplift the race all on their own (Blumin, 1989; Brooks, 1990; Teele, 2002). Approaching issues in this way also leaves fundamental questions about the place of the black middle class in social class stratification unasked and unanswered. We need to know things about blacks that we do not know well for the white middle class: who are they, what sustains them, what is their future, and how are they different, if at all, from other middle classes?

Not Like the White Middle Class

The widespread presence of seemingly well-off and successful African Americans in government, business, and the academy—in virtually all walks of life—may have given most readers the impression that race is no longer an issue in the United States. On the surface it seems that much progress has been made since the 1960s. Many Americans believe the races are now equal and that affirmative action is unnecessary and now disadvantages whites. It would follow from such a belief that color blindness (disregarding race) is the most appropriate way to deal with any remaining racial differences. Pursuing this logic would indicate that poverty among African Americans is no longer the result of racial discrimination and white racism; black poverty would now be seen as self-perpetuating owing to black cultural and psychological inadequacies. The failure of blacks to advance could now be expected to disappear only when blacks decide to address their shortcomings through their own efforts.

The primary evidence put forth to show that race is no longer an issue is the large and seemingly rapid expansion of the African American middle class. William J. Wilson first popularized this point. His book *The Declining Significance of Race* (1978) was based upon his assessment that race as a factor in inequality was declining because of disappearing racial barriers to black upward mobility. Two pieces of evidence are at the core of this view. First, there are descriptions that show the emergence, new affluence, and expansion of the black middle class. Second, there are now hundreds of one-to-one comparisons of whites and blacks in popular magazines and research journals on virtually every conceivable basis. Comparability between the races is controlled by selecting whites and blacks with the same levels of education and income and roughly the same occupations to see how they measure across a broad range of factors. In most cases the comparisons are favorable—both groups are seen as equals.

A Paradox

Even in studies in which black and white middle-class participants have the same income and education and roughly the same occupation, however, there are still persistent and important differences. The two most important differences are in academic achievement and in accumulation of wealth. White middle-class children on average have higher academic test scores and higher academic achievement than black middle-class children (Darrough and Blank, 1983; Fraser, 1995; Gordon and Rudert, 1979; Jencks and Phillips, 1998; Tate and Gibson, 1980). In terms of accumulation of wealth, when nonincome assets such as the value of homes, investments, retirement funds, and regular savings are considered, the average white middle-class family (with class defined as having a college education) has a net worth of $74,922; the nonincome assets of the average black middle-class family (also defined by college education) have a net worth of only $17,437 (Oliver and Shapiro, 1995:94). The average black middle-class families have a net worth that is only one-quarter of the net worth of the average white middle-class families. If the middle class is defined by income or white-collar employment rather than by education, disparity between the white and black middle class still exists. Furthermore, these differences appear to be widening (Oliver and Shapiro, 1995:97).

There are surprisingly few explanations for these and other differences, which suggests a paradox. How can the white and black middle classes be comparable when such fundamental disparities exist? And, more important, how can we hail the end of racially motivated inequality when the class that is indicative of race's declining significance appears to have fundamental inequalities? Quite possibly it is the presumption of sameness between the black and white middle classes that may be incorrect.

Exploring the Paradox

This book has two main goals: (1) an analysis of the presumption of comparability between the black and white middle classes, and (2) an examination of racial class comparability for the other social classes as well.

To accomplish the first goal, I will analyze in detail the presumption of comparability or sameness between the black and white middle classes and will explore this assumption by using a historical perspective. For example, the first black middle class emerged during the Reconstruction period following the Civil War; the second black middle class emerged during the Jim Crow period beginning around 1900—that is, two black middle classes have come and gone, and the current black middle class is the third one. Perhaps examining the history of these first two middle classes will provide some insight into why and how the black middle class since 1970 is, indeed, different from the white middle class. There are undoubtedly many areas that can be compared. We must see whether the routes by which whites become middle class are the same as those used by blacks and whether the underlying structures that sustain the middle class are the same for both races.

Public appearances may hide a world of unseen differences. It is important to ask the same questions about the emergence and vulnerability of the middle class for both blacks and whites and then to compare the two. We need to know what sustains the white middle class and what factors would indicate its decline. And we need to know whether the answers to these questions are the same for blacks. Is the ability of the black middle class to sustain itself based upon dynamics that are the same as or different from those for whites? The point is that the assumption of sameness about the black and white middle classes has prevented such fundamental questions from being asked.

Challenging the assumption of sameness also means having to investigate and think deeply about an additional question. Can two segments of society in the same nation and culture, having such opposite experiences (slave versus immigrant, minority versus majority), enter and participate in the same social class with no underlying differences?

If the answer is, "Yes they can, and have," then different historical circumstances and experiences have had no impact on the present. This is either an extraordinary achievement that deserves much greater attention, or there are fundamental differences and realities that have been overlooked.

In response to the above questions, this book will show that the basic dynamics underlying both the white and black middle classes are the same but that their different historical background and inherited inequalities mean that the dynamics are played out differently. Many people have assumed that everything is the same for both the black and white middle classes, but this is based more upon hopes, sentiments, and ideologies than upon facts. The fact is the experience of the black middle class does not parallel precisely that of the white middle class. Beneath the public image of equality and sameness, blacks are still burdened by historically powerful disadvantages and by present-day inequities. Today, an increasingly blatant racial discrimination exists for the black middle class. In effect, the national racial dilemma has not been resolved, and the presence of a black middle class does not suggest that racial inequality in the United States has ended. Continuing differences in US life are driven by racial as well as social class differences. A central implication of having real differences between the black and white middle classes is that continued inequality between African Americans and whites in the working and lower classes cannot be dismissed as just the problem of the black underclass.

The second goal of this book is to offer a robust examination of racial class comparability. This will show that the black middle class more closely parallels the white *working* class, the black working class more closely resembles the white *lower* class, and there is *no* real black equivalent to the white *upper* class. The absence of a real upper class, despite the evidence of Oprah Winfrey and other wealthy blacks, is an essential difference, with far-reaching effects not only for the black middle class but for all blacks.

A clearer portrait of the white and black middle classes today emerges when one considers experiences and achievements that are intergenerational (across several generations) rather than intragenerational (within the same generation). Looking at the full range of economic and social resources that families lose and accumulate over at least three generations provides a more accurate picture not only of class standing but also of how well entrenched people are in their social class, regardless of race. In this case, black and white Americans in the middle class differ dramatically.

Organization of the Book

What is the middle class? Writers have had difficulty defining the black middle class and are not able to definitively specify who is and who is not middle class. Most simply avoid this messy issue. Social scientists will acknowledge that sufficient income, education, and employment in a specific range of occupations are not the only criteria that distinguish the middle class from others. But then they proceed in their studies as if there are no other criteria.

In Chapter 2, I focus on the definitions of class. The middle class is very much a conceptual moving target, but this is not because of anything inherent about blacks in the middle class. The problem is that the whole concept of a middle class is a conditional and historic one. The problems of defining the black middle class also apply to the general middle class with broader implications about its permanence, size, and stability.

In Chapter 3, we will learn about the emergence of the first black middle class during Black Reconstruction from 1865 to approximately 1890. Ironically, this class emerged from slavery with important industrial skills, property, potential to engage in enterprise, and experience in building institutions. If this class had been sustained without racial restrictions, blacks would have clear advantages over European immigrants who entered the United States after 1900 and whose grandchildren are now the backbone of the contemporary middle class. But this first generation of blacks in the middle class disappeared in the face of a violent southern backlash after the federal government withdrew from southern post–Civil War reconstruction and no longer protected black civil rights during that period. This is why intergenerational upward mobility has been the norm for European Americans from immigrant backgrounds (Clark, 2003; Esslinger, 1975; Warner and Lunt, 1942) but not for African Americans. Events occurring more than 100 years ago have an impact to this day. Few economic and human resources developed by black families in prior generations made it across the generations. Loss of potential intergenerational resources is apparent when we look at the two historic black middle classes that preceded the current one.

In Chapter 4, I will describe the second coming of the black middle class, which developed under more restrictive circumstances after 1900. The turn of the twentieth century was marked by the continued violent expulsion of blacks from valuable property in the South and by a refusal to do business with black farmers and businessmen when they might profit. Whites rioted against black communities that became prosperous. Blacks were lynched—black men for alleged sexual advances on white women; any black person for being financially well-off. Becoming financially independent and living well were considered violations of blacks' "knowing their place" in poverty and subservience. Being economically successful was reason alone for being run out of southern towns. Racial discrimination in southern courts eliminated any possibility that blacks might legally protect their economic progress. Such economic and political disenfranchisement during the Jim Crow period, from approximately 1900 to 1964, left only one avenue for the evolution of a black middle class—to provide services (teaching, preaching, medicine, burying, and sales) to other blacks in racially segregated communities where whites would not provide such services (and would not be allowed to do so even if they wanted to).

Chapter 5 describes the transition to the current—the third—black middle class. Again some history is important. For European immigrants whose grandchildren eventually entered the middle class, work in northern and midwestern urban manufacturing was the basis of upward mobility into the present generation. It was not until World War II, after almost a century of European immigration, that blacks were finally allowed to enter the industrial sector of the economy in large numbers. Shortly afterward, manufacturing jobs went into rapid decline because of plant obsolescence, modernization, and automation. Industry moved out of large cities to the suburbs and other regions in the United States. Industries with well-paying jobs also moved overseas, with businesses seeking more compliant workers who would work longer hours for less pay. It was not that the black middle class voluntarily "abandoned" the black working and lower classes in cities because of post-1965 racial integration. Instead, the economic basis of their small businesses, retail trades, and professional services rapidly eroded after 1960 owing to urban "renewal" and deindustrialization. This same pattern of erosion in self-employed retail businesses and services can be seen today in the wider (white) community. Declining profits and the increasing difficulty of making a middle-class living through retail trade and small businesses and through well-paying union jobs were apparent in black communities thirty years ago.

It is ironic that the differences between the white and black middle classes were better known in the 1930s and 1940s than today. It would have been inconceivable to expect that William Lloyd Warner's 1942 "Yankee City" typology of social classes (reviewed in Chapter 4) would have also described black classes without some differences. Investigators who analyzed the divisions between black classes in the 1930s found them to be so narrow and so fluid that blacks in working-class oc-

cupations would be accepted as solidly middle class if they had the appropriate middle-class values and worldview. If these same working-
class people were white and had the values of the middle class, they
would not have been accepted as middle class by better-educated white
professionals. The black middle class was primarily a class based on
values and affiliations, because the majority of its members had modest
economic resources.

Basic distinctions between black and white social classes were lost
in the post–World War II enthusiasm for quantitative research. Over
time, the complexity of social class was reduced to measures of income,
education, and occupation—the only easily quantifiable aspects of social class. Wealth, the resources of other family members, other inheritances, and values have nearly been forgotten as criteria for defining
and distinguishing social classes. Yet qualitative factors, despite being
complex to measure, also must be taken into consideration to distinguish the black and white middle classes more precisely.

Chapter 6 focuses on the contemporary black middle class. This
class presented new opportunities for primarily working-class blacks to
move up and out into mainstream education, housing, and employment.
Prior to the 1960s, the mainstream of US society had been reserved for
whites. It was through "affirmative action" that a new generation of
working-class African Americans gained admissions to the same schools
as whites, was hired for the same jobs as whites, and was able to rent and
buy homes in formerly white communities. Affirmative action brought
blacks and other minorities into unions, the civil service, colleges and
universities, and private sector jobs, thus partly correcting inequities
from historic racial repression in the United States.

Acting affirmatively then and now is much more than a law, an elite
university's admissions procedures, or a corporation's employment selection practices. Today, the United States Supreme Court's efforts to define the mechanics of affirmative action more narrowly and conservative
efforts to eliminate it altogether apply almost exclusively to the jobs and
circumstances that produced the new black middle class. Affirmative action was initially much more effective as a symbolic and national goal
than it is as a law. More progress was made in racially integrating workplaces and schools through volunteer action than by legal prescription.
In the 1970s, racially integrating one's workplace, college, or university
became the thing to do. Affirmative action is now no longer viewed as
necessary to correct past and current racial inequalities.

The emergence of the contemporary black middle class through affirmative action raises an important concern. Will the gradual elimination

of affirmative action also gradually eliminate the contemporary black middle class? Or has the black middle class achieved a wide enough foothold in the mainstream to be self-sustaining? Unlike the emergence of the white middle class from immigrant upward mobility, two of the three black middle classes required federal action in order to remove racial barriers to their participation in the middle class.

Government policies that created and sustain the black middle class are not without implications for white Americans. At its core, the white middle class may be equally dependent upon federal social policies. Historically, the middle class developed out of personal and family enterprise—small businesses. One would think that this is still the case today. The fact is most Americans now work for someone else, and small businesses are not where the economy is growing and globalization is happening. Like their black peers, the white middle class is increasingly dependent on federal tax policy that permits education and mortgage loans and deductions, federal student loans, the GI Bill, and federal highway funds that made the suburbs possible. The US middle class is also heavily dependent upon domestic corporate investment and the willingness of US corporations to employ Americans rather than cheaper foreign professionals (Glassman, 2000; Zunz, Schoppa, and Hiwatari, 2002).

In Chapter 7, a revision of black social class is outlined that takes into consideration the declining need for black labor, growth of a black underclass, and use of diversity rather than affirmative action to sustain the black middle class. Hip-hop is an important response to the marginalization of blacks from the mainstream economy and has social class implications. All of this is a prelude to what may happen in coming years among white Americans. As there is no longer a need for a large working class in the United States, it is questionable whether there will continue to be a need for a large middle class. Blacks are the first to see the future when we take into account factors such as time of entry into a declining or developing sector of the economy, the presence or absence of intergenerational wealth, time of entry into one's social class, and class-specific social values mediated by lifestyle.

A more accurate comparison of black and white social classes suggests that the existence of the black middle class is hardly evidence of a triumph over racism in the United States. The black middle class is "the last hired and the first fired" in the larger middle class. Whites are still "the first hired and the last fired," but globalization suggests that whites will be fired in turn nevertheless. What is happening in the black middle class and among blacks in general is indicative of rapid changes in the national and world economies and needs to be viewed as such. It is irrelevant to use the black middle class for ideological purposes such as arguing for or against affirmative action or for or against color blindness. The tentative existence of the black middle class is certainly not proof that the US economy and social system are fundamentally fair, when they are not, nor is the black middle class proof that rapid progress has been made in reducing racial inequality.

Chapter 8 looks to the future by addressing several myths about the black middle class (some new and some in review) that stand in the way of a new vision. In truth, most African Americans are part of the working class and underclass. The black middle class has grown out of the working and lower classes as a result of federal policies and is still reliant upon a shrinking working class and federal policies. The black middle class is sustained as a by-product of the increasing dependency of the US middle class on federal and corporate policies. The American dream separate from globalization is over. The fact is that the existence of a large US middle class with blacks as a part of it is becoming increasingly expensive to maintain and unnecessary for continued global corporate profitability—it may simply be running out of time.

If the black middle class declines, so will the white middle class. The only question is, how soon afterward? The difficulties of the children of the middle class, black and white, in maintaining their parents' place in a social class speaks loudly to the growing crisis of the US middle class. The pressure and anxieties are highest in the lower middle class, where most "middle-class" blacks in fact are. The continuing existence of a US middle class, in general, and a black middle class, in particular, may at minimum be dependent upon sparking a new social movement to address economic inequality in US life and in the rest of the world. Such a movement cannot succeed by addressing only racial economic inequality in the United States; it will have to address inequalities among global partners overseas and those inequalities that still exist among whites at home.

2

Putting Class in Context

What does it mean to be middle class? Before one can effectively explore the similarities and differences between members of the middle classes in the United States, one first must review definitions of *middle class*. To do this requires a brief description of how all classes evolved: the historical big picture. The development of classes in the mainstream United States and among blacks does not stand outside of history, as much of what is written about US classes would suggest. So before we consider the two classic definitions of class that are attributed to Karl Marx and Max Weber, we must first review the historical context of both definitions.

Before the Commercial Revolution

Historically, modern western European economies are based upon industry, manufacturing, wage labor, and a dependence on natural resources from overseas. These features became apparent roughly in the fifteenth century (Wallerstein, 1974). Before this time, there were two very clear social divisions or estates that characterized European societies. First, there was the majority of subsistence farmers or peasants who lived hand-to-mouth, producing what they needed to survive. Second, the royal class, which was less than 1 percent of the population, lived by taxing the production and labor of the peasant majority (Palm, 1936). The peasants' belief in the authority and even godlike powers of royalty was intrinsic to the royalty's high social status and its ability to amass fortunes through taxation.

There was a dynamic relationship between the two estates. To make this social order work, however, there had to be a small group in between the royalty and peasants who executed the royal will and ensured the ongoing loyalty and subservience of the peasantry. Someone had to know how to sustain the respect or fear that commoners felt toward the royalty. There had to be people who would be willing to collect taxes, administer the royal treasuries, and use the peasantry to build public works or to serve as foot soldiers in wars. This was the role of the nobility. As intermediaries, the nobility's loyalty, skill, and service were essential to royal survival and prosperity. In turn, those who served as royalty's agents were rewarded with higher social standing and more material wealth than commoners. The middle ranks were supplemented by craftsmen, artisans, and traders who lent their special talents to the acquisition and production of high-quality goods and services for the royalty and nobility. These two small and relatively privileged groups functioned midway between the royalty and the peasant majority.

These intermediaries were essential to maintaining the early social order, yet historically they have received less attention than they deserve. In part, this is because this was a smaller group in number, whose fortunes depended directly on conditions within the two main estates: royalty and peasantry (Hilton, 1985). The wealthier and more stable a royal ruler, the larger and more successful was the middle stratum of nobles and craftsmen. When the royalty and peasantry were in conflict, the middle ranks shrank. They were simply an auxiliary to the ruling class (Boissonnade, 1964). Karl Marx believed that this small group in the middle ranks simply did the royal bidding and, like the ruling class, produced nothing of value. They only benefited from exploiting the labor of the peasantry (Marx, 1967).

Middle Functionaries as a Class

In this early history, tradesmen on occasion became a class unto themselves and used their intermediary roles to advance their own interests apart from the royalty and nobility. As early as the sixth century B.C., traders tried to fracture the power of royalty by making wealth, not birth, the basis of social distinction (Palm, 1936). Based on this concept of advancing the self-interests of middle functionaries, Athens became a bourgeois state, celebrated as the first European democracy. It was not the Greek peasant majority that pushed for democracy: it was Greek traders, artisans, and administrators. Rome was next to transform itself from an empire built on agriculture to one dominated by trade and industry. Again, it was the self-interests of the small middle stratum of traders, merchants, artisans, and administrators that brought this shift about. It is even suggested that the Roman empire fell because the Roman bourgeoisie (middle stratum) refused to open their ranks to subsequent generations of ambitious and prosperous commoners (Palm, 1936). This mistake was fatal, because when Rome collapsed, the fortune and position of its middle functionaries also disappeared.

With the fall of Rome, the Catholic Church became the only organization strong enough to take over the role of government in Roman Europe. Hence, the "Holy" Roman Empire was born, in which the church hierarchy assumed the roles and privileges of both royalty and nobility. In spite of the change at the top, there remained the need for a social stratum in the middle. Several things happened in the European Middle Ages that led to the rise of a new middle social stratum: (1) the royalty sold markets and fairs to commoners to raise money; (2) whole towns were sold in the form of charters to finance the Crusades; (3) the ranks of the royalty and nobility were depleted by plagues, epidemics, and famine; and (4) kings realized that their prosperity, and that of their states, was dependent on having an ambitious and active merchant class (Palm, 1936). Church law forbade profit taking, charging interest, and holding property that did not belong to the church. Twelfth-century Italy became prosperous only because merchants insisted that Roman law be revived so they could earn profits, charge interest, hold private property, and elevate the authority of secular interests over religious rules.

The Revolt and Birth of the Modern Middle Class

By the sixteenth century, the western European commercial middle stratum had become large enough and prosperous enough in its own right to begin a several-hundred-year struggle to free itself from subordination to the royalty and then to challenge and eliminate royalty's power, rule, and hereditary basis of wealth altogether. The next 300 years were characterized by civil wars and revolutions as merchants, traders, and small manufacturers rebelled against royal and noble rule to create national states where trade was free of royal dominance. The landholding and trading populace came to rule through democracy. Only men who owned property (in the middle sector), however, held the right to vote. As European history progressed, the "middle class" assumed greater and greater dominance, pushing royalty and nobility into obscurity, and turning once-revered symbols of wealth into today's European museums and tourist attractions.

It was not sufficient for the middle stratum just to control government. It had to find a way to legitimize its new rule and to gain and retain the loyalty of the peasant majority, whom it needed as a source of labor. Religion had legitimized authority for the royalty and for the politically powerful bishops of the Holy Roman Empire. Now a new validation had to be found. The decisive moment came when Martin Luther advanced his criticism of the abuses of the Holy Roman (Catholic) Church in 1500 and made his call for a Protestant reformation of the Roman church. Fortuitously, he had provided a religious ideological framework that would justify dominance by the new middle stratum.

Luther's revolt is recognized primarily for his assertion that a few men chosen by the Catholic Church and ordained as priests should not be given the power to define everyone else's relationship with God. Ultimately, he believed, one's relationship with God should be dictated by each individual, not by the church. Martin Luther was equally critical of wealthy merchants. He believed members of this class were equally guilty of the abuse of power and privilege so prevalent in his country (Germany). He condemned those who hoarded and monopolized imported goods from the East and who were slowly gaining control of domestic trade as well (Palm, 1936). He believed the nation's temporal existence should not be dominated by the profit making of a few merchants.

It is interesting that after Martin Luther's death, the same merchant class he had criticized co-opted his views and used them to its own advantage. By 1600, the merchant class was solidly behind the "Protestant revolt"; its members accepted that they were "the chosen people" precisely because of their wealth, as best articulated by John Calvin. The wealthier individuals were, the more God had blessed them and the greater the incentive for the peasantry to respect them. In their minds, it was only logical that peasants should submit to the political leadership of those who were more fortunate.

Western European history from the 1500s to the 1800s is taught as successive treatises on promoting middle-class freedoms over the tyranny of inherited royalty and church rule. In reality, however, "we, the people" really meant "we, the landowner and merchant class." In sixteenth-century England, one of the poorest, most populated, yet least tradition-bound of western European countries, only oldest sons inherited their parents' property (primogeniture). There simply was not enough land to go around for all sons to inherit equal shares. Younger sons had no option to stay in subsistence farming on family property: they had to find other land or choose another way to make a living. This presented large numbers of English men options to emigrate elsewhere to farm, to secure military or naval careers, or accept apprenticeships in businesses.

The state of affairs in England was ripe for John Locke's *Treatises on Government,* the first great political tract to represent the position of property owners who had instigated revolts against the nobility. The writings of David Ricardo, Thomas Malthus, and John Stuart Mill also were welcomed by the middle stratum because these authors also argued that it was good for commoners like themselves to acquire capital through trade. They then could invest that capital in mechanizing industries and could profit from finding commercial ways to meet human needs. These authors were convinced that "free trade" was not only permissible but necessary for general prosperity (Palm, 1936). By 1815, the middle stratum of traders and merchants had begun to force its way into the upper levels of English society.

From 1680 on, it was very clear that the middle social stratum was a force to be reckoned with. Its members had formed social and political alliances and had established a consensus that they should dominate government. Their struggles are well known because they were literate and left detailed records of their lives in diaries, correspondence, business records, town directories, and club notes. They self-consciously referred to themselves as "middling sorts" and as a "middling, trading and commercial class." Like their predecessors in Greece, Rome, and the Holy Roman Empire, these middling sorts made their livings as shopkeepers, manufacturers, prosperous artisans, civil servants, professionals, lesser merchants, and the like (Hunt, 1996). Their ability to enter into, respect, and fulfill contracts was central to the group's trade and services. This class of people experienced a rapid expansion because western European economies increasingly required the movement of foodstuff, raw and finished materials, luxury goods, and labor from the hinterlands to rapidly expanding towns and back again.

The values and concerns of this class quickly became apparent. From letters we learn that its members experienced a great deal of anxiety and financial insecurity. Their prosperity and middling positions were completely dependent upon the success of their businesses. And their businesses required sufficient numbers of clients with money who were willing and able to buy their goods or services. Any disruption in their client base, supply lines, or labor force had an immediate impact on their pocketbooks and determined whether they could remain "middling sorts." If their children were unwilling to carry on their parent's business, or an erring son brought shame on the family, a whole lifetime of work could be wiped out (Hunt, 1996). And just as we see today, there was the pressure to outearn and outspend one's middling neighbors and to make one's way into higher levels of the English landowning elite.

The only way to initially escape this stress and adversity was to become an owner of large tracts of land with tenants. The nobility and commoners who were "landed gentry" could generate income simply by renting their properties. The more land they had, the greater their income. This form of passive profit making did not depend on the loyalty of clients. One did not have to worry about the disruption of supplies, intergenerational diligence, the cost of labor, thrift, one's children's chastity, or domesticity. All that mattered was tenant respect for rental contracts. As long as that existed, one could generate income effortlessly over the generations.

Definitions of Class

Max Weber

There is a long history of writers who have attempted to define class. One of the most influential of these writers was a German, Max Weber. He defined class as "any group of persons occupying the same class status," which could be based upon property ownership, lifestyle, or prestige (Weber, 1947:181–182). In effect, as people begin to perceive different social strata, they are tempted to identify where they stand in this hierarchy in relation to others. People form social groups where they have common social affiliations, which can be based upon levels of prestige, specific lifestyles, or property ownership.

Weber's definition of class can apply to any social stratum, but it best captures the ambivalence and instability of those in the middle, where the very wealthy are on one pole and workers are on the other. Membership in the middle class is not based upon some permanently prescribed status such as "royalty" or "commoner." Instead, one's social class is based on a shared perception of one's place relative to all others in society.

Based upon Weber's definition of class, there existed a self-conscious "class" of people who perceived themselves as neither peasants nor royalty. In *Protestant Ethic and the Spirit of Capitalism,* Weber asserted that the values and worldview of this middle strata accounted for the rise of capitalism and the commercial activity associated with it. He described the wealth and prosperity of north Germany and the willingness of its middle stratum to innovate and to take commercial risks. This was in stark contrast to the poverty of the Catholic south in Germany, where people were seemingly unwilling to innovate and change because of church-related traditionalism. In his mind, the social values associated with traditional Catholicism placed moral constraints on all as a precondition for spiritual salvation after death. The newer and more flexible Protestantism emphasized individual development and freedoms.

Karl Marx

By the 1800s, English cities had become centers of manufacturing for world markets. The landscape was dominated by huge factories lacking pollution control and health or safety measures for workers. People experienced seven-day workweeks, with no health insurance, no retirement plans, low wages, long hours, and a dirty and dangerous working environment. Living conditions were no better. The slums that grew up around the factories cannot be imagined by today's standards. People lived in apartments without windows or access to light and fresh air. There were no indoor bathrooms and no running water in tenements. There were no parks, no health facilities, and no schools, because children worked as adults as soon as they were physically able.

At first thousands and then millions of people were dehumanized and exploited by factory owners as low-wage laborers. From the standpoint of factory workers, there was an obvious injustice in this system. The majority of the population had been impoverished through loss of land and loss of an agricultural livelihood, all for the profit of a few merchants and traders. These merchants and traders were often one and the same as the new industrialists.

It was Karl Marx, with the assistance of Friedrich Engels, who described this exploitative system from a worker's point of view (Marx, 1967). In doing so, these two men broke from traditional writings that rationalized, justified, and celebrated the emerging middle stratum. It was clear to workers that the middle stratum no longer functioned as a small group who managed the affairs of royalty and nobility or existed somewhere between the nobility and the majority of peasants. Now there was a small segment of the middle stratum that had replaced the royalty and nobility at the top rung of the social hierarchy, people who had become a ruthless "ruling class." According to Marx, the growing number of middling sorts—these traders, merchants, shopkeepers, clerks, managers, and administrators—were simply extensions of this new ruling class. And just as had happened in earlier history, Marx and Engels recognized that if this new ruling class were wiped out, the "middling sorts" would disappear with them.

Marx asserted in his book *Capital* (1967 [originally published in 1887]) that there were two classes in society that were naturally and permanently in opposition to each other: on one side was the ruling class or bourgeoisie, and on the other was the proletariat or working class. He believed that those who inhabited the middle ranks between the ruling class and the proletariat were of no consequence and merely allies of the ruling class. Marx also described a fourth group, the peasants who were uprooted from their lands by the ruling class and who served as a reserve labor pool. Whenever existing workers demanded too much, they could be replaced by hungry peasants or lumpen proletariat, who would accept even lower wages. Peasants had the same interests as the working class but were not physically or psychologically at the center of the conflict between the ruling class and the proletariat.

Marx was precise about the essential difference between the ruling class and the proletariat. The ruling class owned the means of production (Marx, 1982:271–275)—the factories, mills, plants, plantations, ships, or slaves and whatever else would support profit making. The working class sold their labor for wages. They were employees who worked for a fraction of the value generated from their labor.

Marx did not agree with Weber that classes were defined by inferior or superior positions or merely by different perceptions of status. Rather, he believed classes were based on absolute conflicting interests and fates. For the ruling class to continue earning profits, there must forever be increasing efficiency in productivity, which requires increasing ruthlessness and creativity in exploiting labor. The greater the desire for profits, the harder labor must work, and the deeper people are driven into poverty and desperation. From Marx's perspective, profits and poverty are inextricably linked. The greater the wealth of the few, the greater the poverty of the majority.

Marx contributed greatly to our modern understanding of class. But it is important to separate his theory on class from his role as prophet and icon of western Socialists. From one of Marx's least quoted statements, "I am not a Marxist" (Marx and Engels, 1961), one can surmise that he did not intend for his views on class to be politicized and cast in stone. He understood that class structure and its dynamics could change with time (Althusser, 1969, 1990). As a brilliant commentator for his times, he willingly accepted criticism, revision, and scientific analysis of his ideas. His theory regarding class differences is still very compelling and like Weber's can be updated.

The World Systems Explanation

Studies of the English middling sorts generally neglect to mention that the men in the middle were actually the same men who profited from the exploitation of colonies, slavery in the New World, and the mechanization of crafts. They did not succeed simply because of their diligence and hard work, or because they had the right values, or even because they had God's blessing. Rather, there was a social and economic structure underlying the appearance of this new and expanding class. The growth of the middling sorts after 1680 was in fact directly related to colonial overseas expansion in which England led the rest of western Europe. The English initiated a commercial world system that is unfolding to this day, one that is responsible for creating today's large middle classes in Western Europe and the United States. Here is how the world system developed that is the basis of modern middle classes.

Potatoes were a staple of the British diet in the late 1600s. In the traditional peasant economy, a good harvest meant prosperity and food on the table for another year. But failed harvests meant poverty and starvation. Some enterprising British merchants figured out that if they could devote large tracts of Irish land to potato growth, they could address this cyclical problem. And if they could produce potatoes cheaper than British subsistence farmers, they could sell their product in Britain and still make a profit. When a poor harvest occurred, they would have potatoes to sell when others did not. Their plan worked. With their lower prices and available crops, they drove the higher-priced and less reliable potatoes off the market. Since people would not buy the higher-priced potatoes, the small local farmers stopped producing them. The primary competitors had been eliminated by the new grower-traders. Once they gained control of the local market, they increased their prices and made even more money, because now they had a monopoly on potatoes. They maintained their monopoly by lowering their prices whenever competitors tried to enter the market and by selling below the competitors' prices. Once they had driven the new competition out, they would increase their prices again. These merchant traders became very wealthy by dominating the potato market in England with their Irish-grown potatoes. This became the model for modern economics (Kellen-benz, 1976; Wallerstein, 1974).

This kind of monopoly in production, pricing, shipping, distribution, and sales did not stop with potatoes. These merchants and others soon followed suit with additional commodities. For example, wheat was grown in Poland and shipped back to England. Key to the success of this new economy was growing very large quantities of everyday goods for very little money overseas and then shipping the produce back to one's home country.

There were dire consequences from this new economic scheme. Local British farmers could no longer make their living selling their excess production. As merchants gained control over each successive commodity, farmers were driven out of business and into poverty. Whether in England, Ireland, or eastern Europe, the new economy meant the same degree of local impoverishment. Farmers were displaced from working their own land and forced to toil in cities and in new commercial trades for very low wages.

This is exactly what is happening in the United States today. Although no studies have yet documented what percentage of our consumer goods are being produced overseas, there seems to be widespread agreement that most of them are—at a fraction of the labor costs of production in the United States. Our consumer goods, including food, are then shipped back to the United States for sale at a fraction of what local producers would have to charge. In this sense, globalization is nothing new. Because of much lower standards of living, labor from China, India, and southeast Asia as well as from Central and South America can work for much less than Americans both overseas and as legal and illegal immigrants in the United States. Cheaper labor means lower production costs, which in turn produce higher profits for the businessmen and women who hire the labor and run the businesses. Since World War II, the movement of jobs and manufacturing overseas has dramatically reduced jobs in the United States for high school graduates and those without special skills and training (Bluestone and Harrison, 1982). Now, the same thing is happening to the US middle class: cheaper college-educated and specially trained labor exists overseas that can do many US middle-class jobs.

Historians call the gradual displacement of local peasants by business from lands on which they had survived for generations the "land enclosure movement" (Kriedte, 1983; Wallerstein, 1980). The movement started in Ireland. It is no coincidence that peasants were displaced from their lands in northwestern Europe and then in eastern and southern Europe. The "movement" did not spread because of some force of nature. It was the direct outgrowth of large commercial farms and transnational production and distribution. With the success of this new economy in England, merchants in each western European country adopted the same strategy. By the 1800s the new commercial order had transformed European economies. The "middling sorts" increased in number, and the basis of their very existence was due to the new trade. But in the process of removing royalty and nobility as barriers to their independence and wealth, the middle stratum further impoverished the peasant class in ways that neither the royal tax collectors nor the church could have imagined.

Of course, the new economy antagonized peasants, both at home and abroad. Merchants had to hire small armies to police their plantations and distribution routes. There were additional costs in getting the British government to send troops to far-flung colonies to put down revolts. And there were frequent rebellions during which people damaged plantations and destroyed crops. By the 1700s, England itself was a tinderbox ready to explode. The royalty was waning in power, "middle sorts" were growing in number and influence, and the majority of subsistence farmers were losing their lands. France and Germany, then Spain and Italy soon experienced the same trend. If this new economic approach had been limited to Great Britain and continental Europe, the social costs might have limited its growth and curtailed today's middle class. Instead, the new western European world system grew beyond its internal capacity and survived because it provided an escape for increasingly impoverished and rebellious peasants. Those who escaped emigrated to colonies in North, Central, and South America; Africa; and Asia.

Role of Africans and Beginnings of Race

At first, Spain, England, France, Holland, and Portugal—all the European Atlantic maritime countries—sought control of key trading ports in Africa, Asia, and the Americas. Once established, they used their superior military might to take control of harbors and trading ports. They bribed local royalty and took sides in internal conflicts in order to "buy" native assistance. This is how they got indigenous people to defend and advance European commercial and military interests against neighbors. From these commercial enclaves, local crafts, natural resources, and farm products could be shipped back to the homeland and sold for a fraction of their cost. In turn, finished products manufactured in England, France, and so on could be shipped back to the colonies and sold there at a high price, making profits for the entrepreneurs and taxes for the colonial and homeland government.

To undercut domestic European production costs with colonial products required lots of very cheap labor. The size of one's plantation and the extent of one's profits were limited only by the supply of labor. And labor had to be very cheap to be able to produce, ship, and distribute one's products around the world and still be able to sell the product below local producers' costs. Merchants and planters could not convince enough of their homeland's displaced peasants to emigrate to the colonies. Those who did go initially found life quite difficult. In the Americas, merchants discovered that the Native American population was smaller than expected. The natives did not take to virtual slave labor well and often fled. Using Indian labor also made for poor relations with other local tribes. But the work had to be done. The solution was to resort to slave labor, forcing people to work for a lifetime without pay.

The new economy introduced a further innovation: taking advantage of political and economic turmoil in one part of the world (turmoil that merchants themselves sometimes helped to create) to gain access to a large pool of labor for other parts of the globe. After 1600, west Africa became a prolific supplier of slave labor and overshadowed the older slave trade from southeastern Europe (Davidson, 1961; Du Bois, 1971; Verlindin, 1955; Williams, 1971). For more than 300 years, internal wars between expanding Islamic states and African nations had placed west African societies on the brink of collapse (Williams, 1971). The Sahara desert was physically expanding over areas that once had been fertile, further weakening the African states. Populations that had not been displaced by wars were now uprooted by natural forces. In this troubled environment, Africans captured by Muslims or rival states were sold to western merchants as slaves. Between 1650 and 1880, approximately ten million Africans were shipped to the Americas to grow, mine, and produce every conceivable product for export back to England, France, Spain, and Portugal (Curtin, 1969).

African slaves grew massive amounts of cotton in Virginia, the Carolinas, and Georgia. This cotton would be shipped to England, transforming Liverpool from a small fishing village to one of the largest and most active sea ports in the world (Lloyd-Jones, 1988). Then the cotton would be transported by barges to Manchester, where the first mass production factories of the Industrial Revolution were built. Irish peasants, impoverished by English colonial potato production, were relocated to Manchester and other large English cities to work in the new factories (Hechter, 1975; Rolston, 1993). Irish women and children worked ten-hour shifts, seven days a week, making cloth and other textiles. The finished products were returned to Liverpool and shipped all over the world. British textiles, made from cotton harvested by African slave labor in the Americas and manufactured by Irish workers in Manchester, undercut older cotton growth and textile manufacturing in Egypt, India, and China (Wallerstein, 1974). These other overseas textile manufacturers did not use slave labor, so their products cost more. Textiles became the first worldwide commodity dominated by the British, who made billions in their currency, the pound sterling, in the process.

Emerging Wealth from Trade

There was a dynamic relationship evident here between domestic and colonial trade and the emerging wealth of nations. The larger a country's colonial holdings, the greater its profits and the subsequent wealth for the nobility and middling sorts, alike. The greater the wealth, the larger the army and navy a nation could afford and the more colonies a nation could grab. So a fierce competition developed between western European states over the control of colonies. Without active colonization, a country could not compete in this new world order. A nation could soon fall behind in wealth and military power and easily become a target for domination by a neighbor. From the 1600s right up to World War I in Europe (1914–1917), most of the wars between western European states were fought over control of overseas colonies and trade routes (Cox, 1964; Du Bois, 1945). By the 1800s, England, which had been the poorest and most populated country of western Europe in the 1600s, had become the wealthiest and most powerful nation on earth. It was said that "the sun never set on the British Empire" because England had colonies all around the world.

England achieved this level of dominance because its middle sorts were able to co-opt their royalty and nobility and remove the Catholic Church as a barrier to their interests sooner than other European nations could do so. The English middle stratum increased in number both at home and in the colonies. England also was more willing to export its poor, landless, and potentially riotous population to overseas colonies than were the other western European nations. The English colonies in North America, the Caribbean, Nigeria, South Africa, Egypt, India, Shanghai, and Hong Kong became small replicas of England overseas.

The Development of Class in the United States

The world systems explanation can be seen as an update and extension of Marx's original formulation of the development of social classes. It is not based on Marxist beliefs in dialectic opposing forces or the inevitability of conflict and proletariat dominance. The world systems perspective is not discredited by the abuses of the former Soviet system and its collapse. It points out features of the present modern world economy that Marx could not have anticipated. The world systems perspective in no way refutes or discredits Weber's formulation of classes. As we also will see in Chapter 3, the world systems perspective does not fully explain the development of class in the United States. What neither Marx nor Weber could have anticipated was how important race was to the development of class outside of Europe in the United States, and that the United States would take the place of Great Britain as the economic leader of the western European community. They could not have known how race could be used to obscure who benefits most and is most privileged by the kind of capitalism that goes well beyond national boundaries.

The US experience of class formation is unique when compared to that of Europe. In the United States, race plays a role not just in the development of the middle class but also in social stratification and development of all social divisions—a role that is unimagined in Europe. Whether one believes race is or is not declining in importance today, it was of great importance in the formation of US society in the 1800s and in the early 1900s.

To comprehend the rise and potential fall of the US middle class today, one must look at the role that African Americans played in class development during the 1800s. The nascent black middle class exposes the underlying dynamics and vulnerabilities of middle-class life in the United States. It illustrates the forces that produced a modern middle class and can also cause its demise. The same dynamics of development and then decline did not occur in the white middle class during the same period. The historical literature claims that the US (white) middle class developed during the 1800s and has been in ascent ever since. Some scholars believe there is nothing to learn from the black middle-class experience, because in their minds it was foreign and separate from the mainstream. The unbroken ascent of whites in the middle class may be true, but I do not believe it is true that the white experience is separate and unique from the black experience. Blacks were intrinsic to class formation in the United States and may have mirrored over a century ago the underlying dynamics of class today.

The next chapter looks at the development of the first black middle class and explores the underlying phenomena that both created and destroyed it. My hope is to inform our perspective of the contemporary black middle class and to point out potential risks to the middle-class experience in contemporary society.

3

The Emergence of a
Black Middle Class

The South dominated the American colonial experience and in doing so defined the early basis of class in the United States. English planters, who started off as middling sorts in England, wanted immigrants from England, Ireland, and then other European nations to come to the South. They needed them to offset the large and rebellious slave population. Initially, European immigrants were used as contract and indentured labor to work side-by-side with African slaves. The results were predictable—the immigrants rebelled with the slaves (Aptheker, 1983; Dillon, 1990). To keep poor European immigrants, whose material condition was not much better than slaves, from joining rebellions against the planters, it was necessary to provide immigrants with a higher status and a social identity superior to and apart from the Africans. The initial strategy was to separate Europeans from Africans, to make them think they were superior, and to encourage them to become allied with the planters rather than opponents. How was this achieved? The answer was to invent a racial hierarchy to obscure class differences.

Race over Class

Race in the United States is regarded as conceptually different from class and has been defined at different times as an outcome of human nature, culture, and genetic inheritance. There is even a biblical basis for race in the curse of Cain (Fredrickson, 1971). But race's origin in the United States is really none of these. Its real roots are political; the division of people based on "races" as we know them was created by the

North Carolina and Virginia colonial legislatures in the early 1700s (Allen, 1994; Cecil-Fronsman, 1992). The motivation for this legislation was economic. The races were initially legal entities whose purpose was to protect the power and privilege of planters by elevating Europeans as "common whites" over Africans, who were reduced to chattel slaves (Cecil-Fronsman, 1992). As a result, the European identities of immigrants in the South and in the rest of colonial America became secondary to their American racial identity. It was no longer important in the larger society that they were Irish, German, French, Spanish, and so on. The basis of their acceptance and assimilation as Americans became henceforth as "white" men and women. In turn, anyone of African ancestry ceased being African and legally became part of a separate and inferior status—slave and "Negro."

Race is not apart from class; rather, it is closely related. The incorporation of race into the colonial class system explains the unique features of social class in the United States in contrast to social class in Europe. The end result in the United States is a national system of social stratification different from what Weber or Marx imagined. On the surface, the colonial class structure looks Marxist. There were "white" property owners (a ruling class) with vast landholdings that were certainly the means of production. Then there were all other penniless whites and slaves whose labor was exploited (a proletariat). An ideological Marxist might go no further. But a more in-depth look reveals that southern poor whites were not really a proletariat. Most "whites" were small subsistence farmers, essentially European peasants who were displaced from their land of origin and who emigrated and eventually obtained new land in the colonies. The better off among these farmers may have owned several slaves to produce a surplus for local sales (US Census Bureau, 1979; Guttman, 1976). In North Carolina, the 1860 census showed that out of 630,000 white families, 183,000 owned at least one slave. That means that 71 percent of whites lived in non-slave-holding households (Cecil-Fronsman, 1992). The non-slave-holding white majority ended up serving precisely the role the large planters hoped for. Even though they were poor, they were still "white" and landowners. As long as they held a higher status than slaves, which stabilized the plantation economy, they served as a buffer to keep in check the conflict between slaves and owners of large plantations.

Slavery's Impact on Class

The colonial American system differed from that described by Marx because a larger number of poor whites did not work as wage labor for the big plantation owners. They were not directly exploited for their labor. Thus, there was no "dialectic" relationship (two opposites in conflict with one another), as Marx described it, between poor whites and rich plantation owners. If there was a dialectic and an inevitable struggle, it was intentionally set up between plantation owners and slaves. It was African slaves rather than poor whites who were not compensated for the value of their work. In fact, slavery was an even more complete system of exploitation than Marx had imagined. Slaves received no wages and thus were totally exploited. Furthermore, a person's intrinsic worth and merit, as in Weber's view, did not determine whether he or she was slave or free. It did not matter what values a slave had, because values could not change a lifelong assigned status as "slave." Only the difference between wealthy planters and other whites might be explained by Weber's notion of different values. Furthermore, the planter class remained dynamic in that it was not closed to ambitious new commoners who could get sufficient land and buy slaves. This was an additional incentive to poor whites to defend the system. Any of them could become a rich planter.

Colonial slavery had a great impact on the early development of a middle class in the United States. The planter class, like other elites before them, had need for people to manage their affairs, to serve as highly skilled craftsmen, and to do the planters' bidding. Who fulfilled these roles as middling sorts? In the American colonial system, poor whites were too expensive to do middle functions. Instead, these roles were performed by slaves who were trained as highly skilled artisans and craftsmen. Blacks supervised work in the fields and led work gangs, and some even managed the financial records and affairs of their masters. Not only did slave owners despise manual labor, many considered participation in day-to-day business and trade to be degrading. So slaves tended to these matters and even made profits for their masters (Gordon, 1929). In fact, these slave middle functionaries were so important to the slave owners that there were frequent references to Negro artisans in the wills and inventories of colonial America. Some slaves received substantial industrial training as well (Jernegan, 1965). In contrast, poor whites did what they could: they served as merchants and overseers and policed the roads at night for runaway and delinquent slaves. Most roles and functions done by the middle class in Europe were performed by slaves in colonial America.

The use of slaves to perform middling roles led to a unique consequence: although whites had higher social status, they were effectively locked out of traditional middle-class opportunities to command high wages and to exercise the Protestant values that Weber described. Other than their role of serving as a counterbalance to rebellions and of controlling slaves, poor whites had limited value in the colonial economy. Poor whites were in fact consigned to existing outside the dominant economy; most lived in poverty. Some realized this and continued to align themselves with slaves against the planters (Aptheker, 1983). Virtually every slave rebellion that posed any real threat to the plantation system had white allies and supporters who provided weapons, intelligence, and fellow fighters. But for most whites, there were only two ways to move out of poverty and into the middle class. The first was to jump to the top of the system by becoming a planter, and the second was to move to some other region.

Hierarchy Among Slaves

The southern plantation social structure, which severely limited the development of a white middle class, also made for an odd social hierarchy among slaves. On the surface, there appeared to be two divisions among slaves. The majority were field slaves, whose sole purpose was manual labor to produce whatever their master assigned them to. This was the "class" most likely to rebel. Above them in the slave social hierarchy were the house slaves, whose purpose was to provide for the comfort of their masters and masters' families. A popular belief is that house slaves were less likely to rebel and often had emotional attachments to their masters. But the reality of slavery was more complex and varied and had peculiar contradictions to this image.

A prominent contradiction in the slave system was the "freedmen"—former slaves who lived as "free" subsistence farmers, like the poor whites. It is not clear where they fit in the house slave, field slave dichotomy. There were undoubtedly field slaves who refused to rebel when given the opportunity, a situation that ended up contributing to the collapse of uprisings. The generalization of universal militancy among field slaves is further called into question by other facts. Most slaves did not live on large plantations requiring white overseers where there were clear divisions between house and field slaves. The average slave owner had nine slaves, meaning that the majority of slaves lived and worked on small farms rather than large plantations (US Census Bureau, 1979; Guttman, 1976). So as workers, they had close contact with their masters and did house and field work interchangeably. We should not be surprised that slaves extracted concessions from their masters, because slave owners were dependent upon their slaves and always in their presence. Masters and their families could be poisoned or have unexpected accidents;

valuables could come up missing; secrets and personal habits well known by house slaves could then be shared with field slaves (Aptheker, 1971).

The large numbers of mixed-race children of slave-master parentage made the issue of status and identity among slaves all the more complex. Most mixed-race children remained as slaves according to law, but some were granted privileges and were educated. Still others were set free. There were other bases for distinction and class formation among slaves: mulatto (mixed race) versus blacks, baptized versus non-baptized, "guinea" (African-born) versus slave-born, and free versus slave (Holt, 1977). At some point, and under certain circumstances, all of these divisions were the basis of class and social divisions among slave and free blacks.

The fact is, we can only speculate about hierarchy among US slaves. No single picture of hierarchy or class emerges in the few documents slaves wrote or in materials written about slavery that were not apologies for the system (Blassingame, 1972). Slaves undoubtedly saw themselves as a class apart from and below their masters and other whites, whether they accepted this status or not. Whites undoubtedly saw the distinction between planters and the majority of poor white farmers. The essential point is that the whole social system was set up to make racial hierarchy more important than class divisions. The basic organization of "white" social hierarchy that started in colonial America ultimately shaped and conditioned social hierarchies among slaves and free Europeans alike. The American Civil War was the decisive catalyst in the collapse of the colonial and slave social structure and for the emergence of a modern hierarchy.

The Post–Civil War Social Hierarchy

The American Civil War was not simply a struggle to keep the southern states in the Union, nor was ending slavery its primary reason. The Civil War was primarily a struggle between southern planters and northern industrialists and their respective visions of the nation's future economy (Du Bois, 1935). Until the war, the southern plantation economy had been the nation's primary engine of growth and the center of its wealth. Wealth was generated through slave labor, not through middle-class entrepreneurship or industry. Economically, not much had changed since the nation's origin as a British colony. Cotton, tobacco, and other agricultural goods, which were at the center of the nation's economy, were produced by slave labor and exported to Great Britain for its world trade. After the Louisiana Purchase, the planters expanded into what are now Alabama, Mississippi, and Louisiana. They fully expected that any new western states would also be slave states or, more precisely, extensions of their plantation economy.

The tensions between opposing economic views and ways of life highlighted the contrast between the older colonial class structure of the South and the newly evolving power of the North. What changed was the growing prominence of northern industries and industrialists who envisioned a nation built on manufacturing, internal trade, and industrialization. Their goal was for the United States to become a major world economic power and to use the nation's vast resources and unsettled lands to accomplish this. They could not do this if planters and plantations continued to define the economies of the new states. Northern industrialists, like their counterparts in England, were now strong enough to oppose the old establishment, the plantation South.

The North's victory in the war broke the back of the southern plantation system's dominance of the nation's economy. Planters, basing their wealth on slavery and foreign trade, were eliminated. Northern industrialists became the new dominant class. They now had free rein to expand into the West without competition from the southern way of life or its economic model. The result was a postwar boom in manufacturing and in popular settlements of the West. With this new economic expansion came a rapid growth of the middle functions between the rich and the poor. It was in US cities that new class development and divisions were most apparent during the second half of the 1800s.

In this country, as in Europe, there was a focus on the two most apparent groups. There was a rapid expansion of wealthy industrialists and merchants in virtually every city in the United States (Richardson, 2001). Whole new industries were born. Ambitious, hard-driven, lucky men rose from the ranks of the poor and the near-poor to found and lead these new industries. Family names such as Morgan, Rockefeller, Peabody, and Vanderbilt were associated with entire industries such as railroads, oil, and steel. Then there were the workers, the people employed and exploited by the new captains of industry. These were Europe's displaced peasants who could not be absorbed by industries at home in Europe and whose poverty and numbers left them with little choice but to emigrate to the United States.

Again, the Marxist typology emerges: the rich, capitalist ruling class versus the exploited proletariat. But what was not fully appreciated in the rise of US capitalism and industry in the nineteenth century was the extent to which there were built-in buffers to offset the conflict between capitalists and the proletariat as there were in the plantation South. The movement of enterprise and farming into the interior of the nation produced new opportunities for both classes. There were no limits to business expansion or to employment if you were white. Workers could leave the factory, go west, and resume farming. The "ruling class" also was fluid. With enough money and enterprise, new members could enter this "class" while others who lost their fortunes fell out. The same fluidity existed for the proletariat. As soon as each wave of immigrant laborers learned of opportunities in the West, they left the factories and cities and headed west to grab pieces of the "American dream." The only way industrialists could keep workers was to sponsor successive waves of immigrants. One result is that US workers had higher wages and better living standards than their European counterparts (Blumin, 1989).

Rapid economic expansion, better pay and living conditions, and waves of immigrant workers and laborers who came and went subverted the Marxist dictum of dialectic class struggle. It seemed that Weber's notion of values as an engine of growth was vindicated. After all, under the US system, white people could be whatever they wanted to be.

New studies of this period suggest that older histories underestimated the extent to which this new economic system and rapid economic growth also generated rapid growth of US "middling sorts" (Blumin, 1989). The rush to the farm from the factory turns out to have been an even more extensive rush to the counting room, stock room, clerk's desk, and hundreds of other middle functionary roles. The founding of thousands of small towns in the Midwest and West and the rapid growth of eastern cities speaks to the remarkable expansion not just of industry but also of people performing the work of managing and coordinating the expansion of industry, commerce, and manufacturing.

The Nineteenth-Century US Middle Class

The newly emerging middle class in the United States consisted of business elites, professionals, small-business owners, and "respectable" artisans who lived in increasingly class-segregated urban neighborhoods (Grier, 1988). Captains of industry placed their country estates in what are now the suburbs of US cities. Soon middling folks lived better than mechanics because they could commute to work from the less congested parts of the city (Blumin, 1989). For example, by 1830, 30 percent of Philadelphia's white males listed their occupations as clerks, salesmen, and bookkeepers. And by 1880, manufacturing had replaced skilled manual workers, artisans, and craftsmen, to the point that businessmen and experienced clerks made more money than skilled workers (Blumin, 1989).

The growth of both industrialists and the middle class was so rapid that Stuart Blumin paraphrased Nathan Appleton, an important commentator of the times, from 1844, when he suggested the following: the relatively high wages and unlimited opportunities in the United States seemed to erase distinctions between capitalists and labor and created a society truly ruled by merit rather than birth. So many in the middle class were from labor and immigrant backgrounds that most social and recreational institutions in the 1800s, such as bars, theaters, barber shops, and even churches, were places where people gathered regardless of class boundaries. Furthermore, the growth of the middle class was not without growing self-awareness, an essential Weberian requirement to constitute a class. In 1820, there was little awareness of the rise of the middle class; the older terminology was still used to describe social hierarchy, such as *rank, station,* and *sorts.* In the 1820s, the *Mechanic Free Press* in Philadelphia referred to its relatively well-off constituency as "producers, working men" and as "the working class" (Blumin, 1989). No reference was made to "middle class" or "sorts." But by 1850, George Foster, in one of the first recorded uses of the term, referred to the "substantial tradesmen, mechanics, and artisans of the city" (Philadelphia) as "middle classes" (Blumin, 1989:249).

The main reason for underestimating the rise of the middle class as an outgrowth of the dominance of industrialization and inward national expansion was because rank and "class" differences were not foremost on people's minds. Issues of gender, ethnicity, religion, and especially race were far more prominent (Cecil-Fronsman, 1992). Although nineteenth- and twentieth-century commentaries were celebrating how well-off US workers were and how open were the social classes, the United States was rigidly stratified by ethnicity and race. There were indeed unlimited opportunities from the beginning of the 1800s if you were white and of English ancestry. The earliest industrialists, and those who first joined the middle class, were white, English, and Protestant. Irish immigrants followed native Protestants into the factories and urban sweatshops and were overrepresented as foot soldiers and as casualties in the Civil War. The Irish eventually made their way into the civil services and municipal employment and then into the middle class. They were followed in approximate succession by Germans, Scandinavians, northeastern Europeans, Jews, and then Italians through the 1920s. With each wave of new immigrants came new challenges to English American cultural and political dominance. Particularly problematic were European ethnic groups that were Catholic and Jewish.

It was the way in which these ethnic challenges to Anglo dominance were resolved that is key to setting the stage for racial inequality in the first half of the twentieth century and to the subtle differences between black and white middle classes in the second half. Two things had to happen to each successive wave of European immigrants before they would be permitted out of the underclass, out of the factories and slums, and into the middle class. First, they had to become "Americans," and second they had to become "white." How to become an American is easier to grasp. The United States was an outpost of English culture. To take advantage of opportunities in this nation, English Americans insisted that immigrants learn the English language, preferably convert to Protestantism, and become like English Americans in every conceivable way. Immigrants had to fully assimilate the ways of the dominant English settlers; biculturalism was not an option and was looked upon with great suspicion. The reward for assimilation was economic advancement and acceptance into the middle class. The punishment for resistance was nothing short of economic failure, rejection, and isolation. The first generation of immigrants resisted, but their children assimilated, and each successive generation become more American and less true to its ethnic roots.

Becoming white was not as easily accomplished. Racial hierarchy did not die with the old South. The Confederacy may have been crushed by 1865, but the South's redefinition of Europeans as racially superior "whites" and of people of African ancestry as "Negroes" or "blacks" and therefore inferior was adopted by the rest of the nation. "White" southerners carried their notion of race with them throughout the nation, and their notions about blacks became part of minstrel shows, the most popular form of public entertainment in the United States in the 1800s. Through minstrel shows European Americans learned racial hierarchy (Boskin, 1986; Lorini, 1999). There is no evidence that European immigrants came to the United States with a notion of a black-white hierarchy or racism (Wood, 1995). They learned it here. And like becoming an American, rejecting racial hierarchy and their higher status was not an option.

For Europeans, part of becoming American was to accept that racial identity was more important than one's ethnicity. "All Whites were presumably each other's equal because the only meaningful social distinction was racial" (Cecil-Fronsman, 1992:82). So, whatever one became in the United States, being white was superior to being nonwhite. The research on the development of racial identity is particularly well established for the Irish (Ignatiev, 1995). The fact that European immigrants could be consigned to a social identity as less than "white" (black) was a powerful inducement to rapidly Americanize. Also, a common racial and American identity would reduce any historic enmity between Europeans. Furthermore, without race any religious and historical prejudices among Europeans against each other would be strongly expressed through ethnic urban conflict—Italians were against the Irish, who were against the Germans, and so on. These conflicts were no longer consequential as each group became "white." Regardless of where one's parents or grandparents came from in Europe, being American and white trumped all ethnic identities. Sociologist Pierre Van den Berghe best described this society as a "Herrenvolk democracy" where egalitarian ideas could flourish but were restricted to the dominant caste. In such a system it is predictable that ethnic Europeans would then seek alliances along racial rather than class lines (Cecil-Fronsman, 1992:83).

Was There a Black Middle Class in the Nineteenth Century?

There was another reason for European immigrants to become white. The integration of ex-slaves into US society after the Civil War would have turned prewar racial hierarchy on its head. The most extensively trained and skilled industrial workers in the country prior to 1830 were slaves. Blacks did industrial, skilled manufacturing, mining, steel, and crafts work in the South. After the Civil War, there was no reason for such skilled workers to stay in the South, since there were extensive opportunities elsewhere. Nor was it necessary to induce them to travel thousands of miles across the Atlantic. In most cases, a skilled and available black labor force was only a few hundred miles away from emerging industries in the North and Midwest.

It is hard to appreciate today, but in 1790, African slaves and their descendants were 19 percent of the nation's entire population compared to today's 11 percent; by 1870 they were 36 percent of the population in the South compared to less than 25 percent today (US Census Bureau, 1979). Furthermore, the African population was growing faster than the native European population because of higher fertility and the continuing importation of Africans. Without extensive European immigration and racial barriers, the end of slavery at any time prior to 1865 would have put ex-slaves at the top of the industrial hierarchy by the 1900s because of their numbers and skills. This would have put them in a position to be one of the most successful and well-off ethnic groups in the United States by the time of World War II.

One might wonder how ex-slaves could be ready for such immediate integration into manufacturing and new industries in the North and

Midwest. In the mid-1800s, most workers were unschooled, and most jobs did not require literacy or much more than a willingness and ability to work hard and long hours. Ex-slaves certainly demonstrated those qualities. Entry into the emerging industrial workforce without racial barriers would have set the stage for blacks to move directly into the emerging middle class. Immediately after the Civil War, Black Reconstruction made it clear that there were blacks who were more than qualified to do so.

The Reconstruction Black Middle Class

Just before the attempt in 1865 to reconstruct the South after the Civil War, southern whites put into place Black Codes to continue the subordination of blacks (Foner, 1983). For example, each January blacks had to possess written proof of employment for the coming year. If they left a job before it was over (as determined by their white employer), they forfeited all pay. They were forbidden to rent property, leave their place of work (farm or plantation), or entertain guests where they lived on the plantation without written permission. In addition, they could not pursue an occupation other than farming or being a servant. They could not carry arms and were forbidden from taking timber, berries, fruit, or anything of value from (white) private property. Any violation of these codes was punished by imprisonment. These codes were intended to keep blacks subservient; no middle class among blacks could rise in the face of such laws.

In 1865, General William Sherman, by Special Field Order Number 15, set aside the South Carolina and Georgia Sea Islands for the settlement of Negroes. Each received no more than forty acres. There was a similar experiment in Mississippi at Davis Bend (Stampp, 1965). In 1866, in the first action of the Black Reconstruction, the first Civil Rights Act was passed by the United States Congress and enforced by the United States Army's occupation of the South. It made ex-slaves citizens of the United States and equal to whites in the law, ending the Black Codes (Foner, 1983). For the next eleven years, until the last federal troops were pulled out of the South in 1877, there were attempts at land reform by means of which ex-slaves were given access to land and could vote, hold government office, sue and be sued, testify in court, and experience some measure of physical security. This is precisely when the makings of the first black middle class became apparent. Members of the white confederacy and their supporters were restricted from holding office, effectively keeping the white plantation elite from government. Newly emergent black majority voters in southern states elected blacks to office for the first time. South Carolina had a black lieutenant governor, secretary of state, treasurer, speaker of the house, and associate justice. Mississippi had blacks in the same offices, and a black superintendent of schools. Blacks were in high offices in Louisiana as well (Stampp, 1965).

In 1868, black and white state representatives met in Charleston, South Carolina, to write a new state constitution. The black delegates were lawyers, businessmen, ministers, teachers, former Union army soldiers, and a captain in the United States Navy—all solid middle-class backgrounds. Some delegates had been educated at Eton in England and at Harvard, Yale, and the University of Glasgow (Bennett, 1969). One of the most brilliant of them was Robert Brown Elliott, who was educated in England and spoke French, German, and Spanish. There were similar conventions and delegates in other southern states. Some black delegates had more modest backgrounds than those mentioned: carpenter, blacksmith, coachman, barber, carriage-maker, and waiter. In fact, some of the delegates to the Florida state convention even had to borrow money to get to their convention. The first order of these new state legislatures was to engage in land reforms that turned land over to freedmen, to build and extend railroad lines to stimulate commerce, and to start school systems (most southern states did not have public school systems prior to the war).

Many of the black leaders in 1868 had already been free before the Civil War (Holt, 1977:43). By 1876, 26 percent of all state-elected officials were from freed backgrounds prior to the war. In 1860, seven out of ten free Negroes were mulattoes (of mixed European and African ancestry), but after 1865, six of every ten freed Negro legislators were mulattoes. Only 7 percent of the population in South Carolina was mulatto, but 43 percent of the legislators were. Many in this relatively small group already had land and some capital in livestock before the war. The makings of a post–Civil War black middle class was evident in that 9 percent of Charleston's freed Negro population owned property in 1859, before the war. Of the freed Negroes, 360 owned slaves, with 130 owning an average of three each. Nine owned property assessed at between $10,000 and $40,075, a fortune in those days. This included fifty-four slaves. A number were well educated because their former masters had sent them to school abroad or in the North. There were a number of schools for Negroes in the larger cities of the South, such as Charleston and New Orleans, either maintained in secret or simply ignored because the laws against educating blacks and slaves were not vigorously enforced (Holt, 1977).

Thomas Holt suggested that there was social stratification within the former slave populations, which suggested the makings of an emerging middle class. Mulattoes who held property and wealth before and after the war were at the top. They were followed by non-property-owning skilled artisans who were employed by wealthy whites. Next were former domestic slaves of upper-class white families who were well-off and who had refined lifestyles. At the bottom of the black hierarchy, were freed Negroes who were both poor and unrefined. The majority of nonmulatto ex-slaves was socially ranked below mulattoes; those who owned property ranked over those without; skilled workers were ranked over unskilled laborers; those living in cities and towns were ranked higher in social sophistication and refinement than rural residents. Finally, there was further ranking by church affiliation—Methodists over Baptists, First Baptist over Second Baptists, and Baptists over Pentecostal churches (Holt, 1977).

A unique aspect of the race and class dynamics in the South was how mulattoes, who were obviously privileged during slavery, were not allowed to form a separate identity from blacks after the Civil War or to seek freedom as a third racial group to preserve their higher status over poorer, darker-skinned blacks (although some did for a time in New Orleans before Jim Crow—see discussion in Chapter 4). A number of these wealthy mulattoes were themselves former slave masters who had inherited plantations from their white fathers (Johnson, 1984). Forming a separate privileged mulatto group is precisely what happened in Jamaica, Haiti, and, to a lesser extent, Brazil. Mulattoes in the United States had to choose instead to identify with blacks, as whites would not permit the mulattoes to be identified as anything other than blacks. A cornerstone of southern and now US belief is the necessity for maintaining white "racial purity." By virtue of having any African ancestry, mulattoes were black and were to be treated as such. The absoluteness of US racism cut off any possibility of a third and intermediate identity for mulattoes. Despite mulattoes' ambivalence about race, the majority of ex-slaves went along with their leaders but was, nevertheless, very mistrustful of them.

It was during Black Reconstruction that the first "affirmative action" measures were taken in the United States. Efforts were made to integrate blacks into jobs that had been restricted to whites, such as postmasters of rural post offices, sheriffs, tax collectors, and voter registrars. The South Carolina legislature established scholarships for Negro students to attend the all-white University of South Carolina. Then in 1873, the same legislature had to provide additional support after many white students stopped attending the university (Tindall, 1966). Blacks who managed the affairs of former masters and planters started their own businesses to market goods and provide services to blacks and whites alike. But most important, it was during this period that blacks were granted unsettled lands and tracts of large prewar plantations to begin lives as independent farmers. All the skills and human resources acquired during slavery before the war, especially those that served middle functions, came into view during Black Reconstruction. A black middle class that fulfilled the Weberian criterion of consciousness of self was very much in the making; evidence of their consciousness and unity was in political activism in their own self-interest. Among these upwardly mobile blacks, there was extensive social organization around churches and fraternal societies, a number of which had existed during slavery.

For the Reconstruction black middle class, their rise above the masses to the middle class was not a result simply of doing valued work that others could not do. For both the white and black middle classes, Anglo conformity was essential. Reading, writing, speaking Standard English, having refined manners, and being courteous were important markers of higher status. To act middle class meant one could go into the company of higher-class people and be accepted rather than embarrassed. Black and white members of the middle class could easily recognize each other from their common Anglo conformity. But Anglo conformity is where the similarities ended and the differences began.

First, a behavioral criterion for class standing was more important among blacks than whites. They had little else. Second, the black middle class was just in its first generation, thus only mulatto members had any long-term experience with privilege. Whites who were in the middle class for the first time did not come out of slavery, nor did they have racial barriers to their upward mobility. In contrast, by 1880, blacks were only fifteen years out of slavery. Third, most blacks in the middle class were there by virtue of their own education, skill, and enterprise and because of the civil rights legislation in the postwar South. With the exception of the mulattoes, who had been sent away for education by their owner-parents, none had financial or educational resources inherited from a prior generation.

There was another subtle difference between the black and white middle classes in this period. The ascending black middle class could not become white; only European immigrants were granted that privilege. This final barrier was not just a matter of lacking civil rights and cultural exclusion. For many blacks the presumption of white superiority and black inferiority became a psychological mark of inferiority that was internalized. They may have felt superior to other blacks because of their higher class standing, and if they were mulatto, they may have felt superior because of their lighter skin color. But whites considered them all to be inferior. Whereas aspiring Europeans were accepted into the middle class, claims of Anglo conformity, bourgeois morality, and occupational and educational status by blacks were not just roundly rejected; they were mocked. The minstrel shows were relentless in mocking and parodying black people dressed in middle-class clothes and "putting on airs." All that constituted being middle class was equated with whiteness, and blacks were not white and were incapable of being white. Black claims and desire for middle-class status were viewed as futile desires to be white (Gaines, 1996).

The reaction of blacks whose claims to social status were absolutely rejected in the larger society was to work toward creating an alternative and separate social identity and community. They organized separate communities and social worlds to shield them from "white" presumptions of black inferiority. In contrast, whites who aspired into the middle class could be rejected because of their ethnicity or religion (being Catholic or Jewish), but once they forgot or hid their ethnicity and religion and acquired enough Anglo conformity, they could pass into the mainstream. They did not have the constant challenge to create a subcultural alternative to shield themselves from a presumption of inferiority held about them in the larger society.

Finally, there is the most important distinction of all. The black middle class came into existence and survived because the federal government enforced civil rights laws, held remnants of the declassed white plantation owners and confederates at bay, and guaranteed white and black political equity—one person, one vote.

During the Black Reconstruction, blacks clearly thrived and produced a small middle class. But soon after the Freedman's Bureau was shut down in 1869 and federal troops were withdrawn in 1877, the ascendancy for these blacks was quickly reversed. The convict-lease system was started in which any black person jailed for any reason was leased out by the state to work for private employers without pay. Blacks were again excluded from juries; black sheriffs and police were removed; and poll taxes (for blacks) were instituted (Foner, 1983). After the 1878 elections, blacks could not gain any more legislative seats. In 1882, South Carolina passed new registration and election laws to disenfranchise blacks (Tindall, 1966). George Washington Murray was the last black man to represent South Carolina in Congress; he remained in Congress until 1895. The last black postmaster was the South Carolinian Frazier Baker, who was appointed in 1898; he was shot to death, and his family was burned alive in their home (Tindall, 1966).

Why were the Black Reconstruction and its promise so quickly ended? C. Vann Woodward suggested that it was because of northern racism; white government and business interests would not champion blacks against other whites for very long after the war (Woodward cited in Richardson, 2001). Others have suggested that northerners were exhausted after the Civil War and were turned against blacks by reports of corruption in the Black Reconstruction governments. A subsequent historic examination found that this latter claim was grossly exaggerated. Another explanation is that northern leaders perceived a major conflict between their agenda and that of the Reconstruction leadership (Richardson, 2001). The industrialists favored a harmonious economic world based on free labor, whereas the Reconstruction leadership favored land reform and continued use of government to produce equity between races and classes. Black Reconstruction leaders not only advocated that one race should not have a built-in advantage over another but also believed that no class should have advantages over the other by virtue of controlling the government or the economy. The majority of blacks supported these views.

It turns out that Reconstruction leaders championed ideas feared by northern industrialists who recognized that blacks could be the most senior of workers in their industries. If blacks made the same demands in northern factories that they were making in the South, there would be serious conflict between workers and the owners. The bottom line was that by 1895, the Black Reconstruction gains had been wiped out along with the first black middle class, and the majority of blacks were literally "locked down" in the South while the industrial economy flourished in the North and Midwest with European immigrant labor.

Lessons Learned

What can we learn from this brief appearance of a black middle class and the dynamics of class in the United States in the 1800s? First, there are conditions and circumstances that allow a middle class to emerge, to sustain itself, and to end. The middle class is not the outcome of some natural state that stays in place for those who work hard, achieve, and have appropriate values. If there is enough violence and threat directed against those who are assuming the middling roles, a middle class will not form, nor will it continue if it already exists. Since the US white middle class is in its second century of ascension, it has no historic experience with conditions that can end its existence.

The second lesson is that a middle class as we know it is not necessary for the social system to function. A small elite can maintain a reasonably stable social system with an extraordinary amount of inequality by having functions historically done by a middle class performed by slaves or cheaper labor. The white middle class was retarded in the South by the slave-holding elite's willingness to train slaves to perform highly skilled functions. The granting of racial rather than class privilege retarded the development of a vibrant middle class and kept southern whites in abject poverty while they defended the slave system. Race was used to unify Europeans and to frustrate the development of class interests that would have been critical of the plantation elite.

The third lesson is that entry into the middle class is not based solely on the extraordinary efforts of rare individuals. When conditions allow and opportunities develop, groups of people move into the middle class based on human and material resources they already have. Opportunities must coincide with personal ambition, which results in the growth of a middle class. But clearly when the opportunities disappear, no amount of personal ambition can in itself change one's class or maintain that class for most.

The final lesson in the experience of the first black middle class is that one becomes and remains middle class at the pleasure of powerful elite interests. The measures that permitted the Black Reconstruction middle class to form were federal laws (Civil Rights Act of 1866) and the enforcement of these laws by federal troops. When the troops were withdrawn and the law was no longer enforced, violence against blacks mounted, and whites had no need to enter into or to honor contracts with blacks. The conditions disappeared to sustain the continued existence of a black middle class.

One could argue that all of these lessons are apparent in the long European history of the middle class, as reviewed in Chapter 2. But none of these lessons is apparent based solely on the experience of European Americans in the 1800s. The unbroken ascent of the US middle class during that century provided no guidelines. One has to turn to the depression of the white southern middle class during slavery and to the rise and fall of the first black middle class to see the conditions and vulnerabilities of the general middle class in life in the United States.

In the next chapter we will learn more about the conditions that create and sustain a middle class by looking at the emergence of a second black middle class.

4

The Class That Jim Crow Built

After Reconstruction and the withdrawal of federal oversight in 1877, the methods for political disenfranchisement of blacks were ingenious. There were literacy tests to prove to white voter boards that black registrants could recite and write any section of their state constitution— something board members could not do (can you do this?). One black candidate for the 1890 election was refused certification because his ballot was the wrong size and color: not white paper but white paper with a distinct yellow tinge (Foner, 1983). Blacks were run out of political office based on false charges of corruption and abuse of powers. Violence was used to force other blacks from government jobs and law enforcement positions. Blacks also were found unqualified for jury duty, especially in trials with white defendants. Where blacks were a majority of the voting age population, as in Mississippi and South Carolina, disenfranchisement was particularly harsh.

Under no circumstances were blacks ever again to be the political equals of whites, to govern whites, to define how the state would run or what its mission and responsibility to the public would be. The white historian John Burgess referred to Black Reconstruction as "the most soul sickening spectacle that America has even been called upon to behold" (quoted in Stampp, 1965:6). The brief post–Civil War period of equality for blacks was completely repudiated. Any circumstances in which blacks were equal to or superior to whites, whether it was in business or whether they owned more or better property, was unacceptable and violently opposed. In 1896, the United States Supreme Court formally ended any pretense that blacks had the same rights as whites to participate in US society when it handed down the *Plessy v. Ferguson* decision. Blacks were consigned by law to a world that was separate from and "equal" to that of whites. According to the Supreme Court, racial segregation was legal and not against the US Constitution.

After 1896, the post–Civil War experiments in restricting blacks were consolidated into Jim Crow rules (the name Jim Crow was taken from that of a character in a song-and-dance act). These rules became the accepted etiquette in the new century. Jim Crow was an elaborate and comprehensive system of racial oppression in which blacks were to acknowledge at all times their inferior status in every social interaction with whites. White men, regardless of class and condition, were addressed as "mister" and white women as "miss" or "missus," whereas black men and women, regardless of class or age, were addressed as "boy" and "gal" or by their first names. Blacks were "nigra," "niggers," "coons," and "darkies." Black men and women had to give way to whites on sidewalks and roads. They could never argue with or raise their voices to a white person. And under no circumstance were black males beyond the age of puberty to even look at a white woman directly. Blacks had to hold their heads down and avert their eyes to avoid being accused of insolence. Violate these norms, and one was beaten at best or lynched, castrated, and burned at the stake at worst. It is important to acknowledge, however, that the Jim Crow system was not omnipresent through the South: it was more extreme where blacks lived in greater numbers and less so in cities and where fewer blacks lived (Woodward, 1966).

From the 1890s through the early 1960s, lynchings claimed hundreds of black lives each year. Between 1882 and 1968, it is estimated that 4,742 blacks were killed by lynch mobs; thousands more were murdered by individual whites, by "nigger hunts" during which victims' bodies were dumped into rivers and creeks, and by legal lynchings—speedy trials with legally sanctioned executions (Litwack, 2000:12). To kill their victims was not enough. Lynchings were public theater where victims were tortured for the amusement of the crowd; newspapers even announced in advance the time and place of lynchings. Special excursion trains were chartered to take spectators to the sites. Employers released their workers early, and parents wrote notes to excuse their children from school so they too could attend (Litwack, 2000).

The experience of Anthony Crawford is a good case in point. To paraphrase Leon Litwack, Crawford was born of slave parents, had twelve sons and four daughters, was secretary of the local African Methodist Episcopal church, and was a substantial landowner and farmer in Abbeville, South Carolina. Crawford came to town to sell his cotton and ended up exchanging harsh words with a local white businessman over a price for his cotton. After being beaten by a white mob, Crawford was arrested and placed in jail to keep him from being killed for his insolence. When he was released, the mob attacked him again, put a rope around his neck, and dragged him through the streets of the Negro quarter of town as a warning. They finally hung him to a pine tree and emptied their guns into his body. The newspaper account gave the following reason for his murder: "Crawford was worth around $20,000 and that's more than most white farmers are worth down here. Property ownership always makes the Negro more assertive, more independent, and the cracker can't stand it" (Litwack, 2000).

Attempts to destroy blacks' aspirations to improve their lives and circumstances were particularly thorough in the rural South, as the Crawford case shows. But the Crawford case was not unique. The historical record is less forthcoming about the extent to which blacks who owned valuable and productive property were driven off their land by whites who wanted to seize it. Blacks fleeing to Kansas from the South told of whole black communities being driven off their land. For example, six black men in Mississippi rented a plantation and worked it with their families. After the harvest, the white owner made claims that the black tenants' debt exceeded what was owed them. So the owner took 700 bushels of wheat, corn, their hogs, and a wagon with horses from them. The farmers went to court to protest but without success. Shortly afterward, "masked regulators" took the men from their beds, hung them, and lashed their bodies to boards that floated down the Mississippi River (Guttman, 1976).

Then there were the Howard County riots of 1883. Part of Howard County, Arkansas, was what one white militiaman called "a perfect Africa": prosperous and all black. Two black brothers had a dispute with a white neighbor who wanted their land. After the argument, the white neighbor attempted to rape one of the brother's daughters. A lawyer refused to take the case, and the sheriff refused to arrest the neighbor, saying that it would only cause trouble. The father convinced other black men in the community to go with him to arrest the white man, who fled after a gun battle. Soon a large group of whites pursued the black men, who could not be dislodged from one of their farms. The state militia was called in. Regardless of whether they were involved or not, all of the black men in the community were arrested, including boys and old men. Forty-three went to jail—ten were acquitted. All of the imprisoned men's families had to sell everything they owned for little to nothing and leave the community (Guttman, 1976).

There were untold incidents of white night riders who visited prosperous black farmers, threatening them if they did not leave, raping the farmers' wives and daughters, and then burning down houses and barns for good measure. The impact of this history is with us to this day in traumatized black family systems. Many black students in my African American Families course—the first in their families to attend college—have been shocked after doing family histories and genealogies. A number found that their families had once owned substantial property in the South that is now very valuable. They learned that their families had been driven off this land by members of the Klu Klux Klan and night riders. After fleeing, often in the middle of the night, family members would end up in southern cities and eventually migrate to their present homes in California and other states, where they have lived in poverty.

Impacts of Oppression

Memories of the lynchings, rapes, and burnings have been deeply buried and kept as family secrets among these students' elders. Many students found out that one or more of their relatives had been lynched or a great-grandmother and her daughters had been raped by night riders. The lynchings of their relatives sometimes were covered in the local newspapers, but the rapes were only evident in family members who afterward were mysteriously light skinned. Before learning their families' histories, students had thought the frequency of female-headed households was due strictly to poverty and lack of education in their parents' generation. They were surprised to learn that prior to the incident, whether in the 1890s or 1930s, their families were intact and had husbands and wives across at least two previous generations. After the incident, however, the family culture reflected and protracted the trauma. For example, in one family, women socialized their daughters in subsequent generations to believe that men could not be expected to care for or protect them. Men reared in these traumatized, female-headed families felt a particular need to demonstrate their manhood and were in and out of jail for various violent and antisocial acts. No one in the subsequent generations after the incident was aware of the source of this socialization from earlier generations.

The rise and fall of the Reconstruction black middle class was decisive in the development of black social class and of a new middle class in the 1900s. Carter G. Woodson reported that many of the Reconstruction political leaders and businessmen fled for their lives into southern cities or into the North as the first black migrants (Woodson, 1918). Any blacks in rural areas who were well-off or outspoken or who had gained privileges during black Reconstruction were the next to go. A large proportion of these two groups were mulattoes. This meant that black farmers who owned their own land held the top position in the black class structure, and, as we have already seen with Anthony Crawford, this made them completely vulnerable to white violence. Skilled artisans and domestic servants who did not own land continued to be employed by wealthy whites and, by virtue of their employers, were somewhat protected from white violence. But the majority of blacks continued to be poor, without property, education, or protection.

It was only in large southern cities such as New Orleans, Charleston, and Atlanta that elements of the deposed black middle class maintained any presence. But even there blacks were not safe from periodic urban pogroms. White fears of blacks followed them, shifting from rural to urban communities: "Fear of urban black men and miscegenation were further stroked by the image of the rootless, underemployed 'worthless Negro' of southern towns, a monstrous image that was central to the journalistic and social science representation of urban pathology and mulatto degeneracy" (Gaines, 1996:72).

White fear was occasionally acted out in mob violence when whites invaded urban black communities to rape black women and burn property, especially if the black area became prosperous. In the urban pogroms, the property of prominent blacks, in particular, was targeted. In 1906, W.E.B. Du Bois's daughter had a special hiding place in their Atlanta home in case of white mobs, and she had to use it. By 1921, the black community in Tulsa, Oklahoma, became one of the most prosperous in the nation, until it was burned to the ground and its prominent citizens either run off or lynched. The violence was targeted particularly at people who could assume the traditional middle-class functions.

Impact on Culture and Psyche

In response to the functional loss of a middle class, black aspirations for a better life were channeled or expressed in ways that would not threaten southern whites. Community improvements such as installing sidewalks or street lights or providing city services such as water or police protection could not be obtained through political officials. Blacks were powerless. Starting any business that could be viewed by whites as "uppity" or too successful was avoided. Most blacks instead turned to purely social activities and to their churches. Powerlessness was channeled into after-church social events, frequent extended family gatherings, church picnics, and excursions to other churches, towns, and recreational sites. Before Jim Crow fully set in, black church groups even chartered special trains for their visits (Tindall, 1966). In addition to the church, the better-off members of black communities had lodges, fraternities, sororities, burial services, and other social societies.

The impact of political disenfranchisement was felt right down to the community level. Leaders were powerless and exposed and also could not be protected from white violence. Schoolteachers rarely became community leaders despite their education, as they could not keep their jobs if they offended their white employers. Black preachers were not directly dependent upon whites but were also endangered. Many resorted to emotionalism and religious fundamentalism to avoid having to face their powerlessness. Black businessmen rarely stepped outside of their role because their livelihood depended upon white patronage, good will, and protection (Newby, 1973). Only the National Association for the Advancement of Colored People (NAACP), founded in 1909, was in a position to challenge racist laws and practices. This was because the organization's leaders were based in northern cities, safely away from the day-to-day white violence and control in the South.

A "Middle" Like No Other

A lack of political power forced blacks to limit their aspirations primarily to business and other professions that served only blacks. This would minimize any threat whites might feel. After 1890, a new black middle class arose that would not compete with whites or have any presence in the broader community, in contrast to the prior one during Black Reconstruction. In one of the few surveys of black businesses in the Jim Crow South, an investigator found that in 1927, only forty-nine black-owned and -operated "major" businesses existed in South Carolina. On average these businesses had three employees, most of whom were family members, and they paid on average from $180 to $1,168 in total weekly wages. Only a couple of businesses were sizable enough or profitable enough that they would have been considered major if they had been owned and operated by whites. Seventy-five percent of their patronage was blacks, and whites made up the rest of their clientele. Virtually all of these businesses were in the state's four largest cities—Charleston, Orangeburg, Columbia, and Greenville. These businesses fell into the following categories: undertaking, banking, insurance, tailoring, grocers, shoeshine parlors, dry goods stores, shoe repairers, real estate, dry cleaning, laundering, and cafes. The study author did not provide the name of a single business but instead described them only in generic terms, as at that time it was too dangerous to identify them by name (Gordon, 1929).

A peculiar system of social class developed among blacks that neither Marx nor Weber could have anticipated. The "means of production" and control of the state were monopolized by race, not by class. All blacks, regardless of class, were relegated to an inferior caste. According to Weber, possessing a work ethic that emphasized personal enterprise was the basis of wealth. Blacks were barred from expressing such values outside of their own communities, however, so their aspirations could be expressed only among other blacks. The results were devastating. Blacks were kept from starting businesses of any regional or national significance, were kept out of middle-class jobs outside of their communities, and were barred in large numbers from the rapidly evolving industrial economy until after World War II. Under Jim Crow, the shape and form of black inequality were fixed well into the new century.

Impact on Whites

Blacks were not simply "put in their place." A new system of white racial supremacy was invented during Jim Crow that did not require slavery. Blacks became a caste-class in the new century. By permanently consigning blacks to the bottom of the social hierarchy, all whites were elevated in class status and material conditions. Because of their race, whites were automatically of higher status than blacks and could expect full privileges when it came to jobs, housing, schooling, and public accommodations. There would be no white lower-class equivalent to that of being black. For this reason, working-class and even poor whites regarded themselves as "middle class" early in the twentieth century, even when they had little material or social foundation to think of themselves as such (Baritz, 1989).

It is not surprising that the new system of racial superiority during the Jim Crow period retarded southern economic development. With up to 50 percent of a state's population prevented from advancing economically, it was to be expected that the larger state economy would be retarded as well. So states with a high proportion of blacks in their population (South Carolina, Mississippi, Alabama, and Louisiana) never fully recovered economically from the Civil War. To this day, they have the highest poverty rates in the Union (US Census Bureau, 2006). The end product of Jim Crow was the creation of the most thorough system of racial oppression ever devised outside of slavery. This system was studied and partly copied after 1932 by the Nazis to control "inferiors" in Germany and after 1950 by the Boers of South Africa in setting up Apartheid (Cell, 1982; Kuhl, 1994). Despite the fact that millions of Europeans lost their lives and thousands of US soldiers died to end Nazism in World War II, the US prototype of Nazi racial oppression survived for two more decades after World War II until it was dismantled by the federal government. It was only the voluntary end of Apartheid that narrowly averted a bloody civil war in South Africa, which would have had direct implications for the balance of powers between the West and the Communist world.

Even into the present, whites have been affected in another way by the Jim Crow period. The model of today's US conservatism was first articulated by southern white politicians to rally poor whites against blacks and to malign the goals of black Reconstruction politicians to rebuild southern states and create a racially equitable society. Strong states' rights are an interesting carryover from the Jim Crow period into contemporary conservatism. Conservatives believe that states should have the power to define their internal affairs without interference from the federal government. This was the justification used for getting federal troops out of the South to end black Reconstruction. The call for states' rights was used during Jim Crow to keep the federal government from interfering with southern States' violation of blacks' civil rights. Today's conservatism parallels the Jim Crow period in another way. Conservatives believe that the larger the government, the more oppressive it is and the more it will interfere with individual liberties. In the past, night riders and Klansmen could operate without outside interference when the federal government was too weak to meddle and when these groups actually controlled state government. Whites with local power who saw black civil rights as a threat to their privileged positions could very effectively use extralegal means to enforce their will—in particular, violence.

In contrast, Reconstruction governments led by middle-class blacks raised taxes for public works, made whites and blacks equal under the law, started public schools for blacks and whites alike, and generally interfered with whites' "privilege" to do whatever they wanted to blacks. White "conservatives" knew that a weak state or federal government could not intervene. Also a federal or state government in extreme debt does not have funds to enforce existing laws or to create and enforce new ones.

Contemporary conservatism, like its Jim Crow ideal, believes there should be harsh penalties for violating laws. In the Jim Crow South, that meant harsh penalties against blacks who violated laws but lighter penalties for whites. Laws were designed to keep blacks subordinate. Once in jail, blacks were expected to work in convict-lease programs for no wages. Whites held the belief that law enforcement was necessary to control blacks because there were so many blacks who were unwilling to accept subordination.

During slavery and then Jim Crow, it was a white man's right, even his duty, to carry a weapon. Where whites were in the minority, or at least felt they were, they believed it was essential to be well armed at all times in case they had to forcefully and immediately deal with any threat to white authority. This anxiety and feeling of being threatened still exists and can only be addressed by being well armed. Also, today one frequently hears the conservative doctrine that family is foremost. The same belief was held during Jim Crow, but it meant more than the words imply. Preserving family meant protecting white women from black men who allegedly lusted after them and who, if given a chance, would wreak havoc on the white race and produce a nation full of mulatto children.

In the US cultural context, these race-coded ideals distort white thinking about politics, privilege, and economy to this day (Bowser and Hunt, 1996). Older white voters are easy prey for politicians who use fear of blacks and of black control over their lives as a way to get elected and reelected. Fear of black control also keeps many whites primarily focused on race and mindful of the presumption that whites are supposed to be better off than blacks. So knowledge, awareness, and a willingness to act on class interests among middle- and working-class whites are as retarded today as they were during slavery. The richest 1 percent hold one-third of the total wealth of the national economy (Cagetti and Nardi, 2005) and in doing so heavily influence control of the rest by manipulating democratic government in their own interest with little criticism or opposition from middle- and working-class whites. They can do this because it is more important to maintain white racial unity in the face of an alleged black threat. In effect, the Marxist perspective on class struggle and the idea of a ruling class have been obscured almost completely by race.

Arising Out of Nowhere

The history of the Jim Crow period was not written with class differences in mind. But one thing is clear: disenfranchisement of blacks eliminated three of the five social requirements for the development of a middle class, which are a central government, presence of political and religious tolerance, absence of war and violence, stable currency, and an adequate transportation system (Grayson, 1955). First, for any middle class to develop there must be a central government that can maintain law and order so that trading can take place and contracts can be entered upon and executed. Under Jim Crow, blacks were placed outside of laws regarding trade and contracts. Whites did not have to honor any social or business contract with blacks for exchange of goods and services because blacks had no recourse to the law. Whites could pay black merchants, farmers, and service providers whatever they wanted, when they wanted, if at all. Second, a middle class must have a reasonable measure of political and religious tolerance to exist. When blacks were forbidden to participate in government, they were unable to influence government or use political leverage to protect their property, businesses, persons, or trade. Third, a middle class cannot develop amid war or violence. The Jim Crow period was characterized by pogroms against small southern black communities and intense violence against aspiring blacks:

> The violence inflicted on black people was often selective, aimed at educated and successful Blacks, those in positions of leadership, those determined to improve themselves, those who owned farms and stores, those suspected of having saved their earnings, those who had just made a crop—that is, black men and women perceived by Whites as having stepped out of their place, "trying to be white." (Litwack, 2000:30)

The measures taken to end Black Reconstruction and to keep blacks subservient were particularly aimed at eliminating and preventing a middle class. As was pointed out earlier, those who tried to advance were targeted in particular. It seems, therefore, that the only conditions required for an emerging middle class that were not in question were an adequate and stable form of currency and sufficient transportation for trading goods and services.

Despite white violence and the elimination of the Black Reconstruction middle class, black aspirations and efforts to improve themselves did not end. The freed black property class was replaced by a segregated service middle class. One had to look to large cities, places of black refuge, to find evidence of a reemerging and second black middle class. Jim Crow was somewhat mitigated in the larger cities of the South (Wade, 1964). It was harder to enforce racial restrictive laws and practices in urban communities, and for blacks it was easier to remain anonymous and escape the day-to-day threat and random white violence. Although these racial ghettos received few, if any, city services, there was safety in numbers. White night riders could not terrorize urban blacks as easily nor conduct pogroms as they did in rural areas and small towns because urban housing was closely packed, unlike rural tracts where people lived in isolation from one another. In cities, night riders were met with stiff and determined opposition. Blacks maintained guns and fought back. There were only a few places where Jim Crow could be rigidly enforced in cities. They were in employment, where blacks did the hard, dirty, lowest-paying, and most dangerous work; in housing, where there was rigid racial segregation; and in public accommodations. Blacks had to use the back doors of white businesses if they did not have a separate "for colored only" entrance and had to ride behind whites on buses and in separate train coaches behind the engine or at the end of the train.

It was in this context of racial segregation that a small black service middle class arose. Since whites would not and could not provide personal services to blacks, it was open to other blacks to provide the full range of services that were needed: barbering, hair care, construction, repairs, medical, dental, pharmacies, grocery stores, clothing shops, restaurants, bars, and cafes. In playing these roles, blacks created a world of professional, commercial, and personal services parallel to the white world. So the white middle class served whites, and the black middle class served blacks. In time, small middle-class residential enclaves developed in black communities.

Under Jim Crow, most blacks came to emphasize social life within their segregated worlds and left political and economic issues alone. Others started social movements and became activists on a variety of fronts to uplift the race. In order for black people to get background training and skills to fulfill professional and craft roles, more than ninety black colleges, universities, and technical schools were started to supplement the dozen black colleges started after the Civil War and during Black Reconstruction. Graduation from these schools was an automatic ticket into the black middle class, and these institutions were the source of activists for further improvements.

Members of the Jim Crow service middle class could not become part of the white upper class nor form an upper class with the same material and political basis as whites. What constituted the black middle class during Jim Crow was severely limited and frequently under assault. The result was that blacks formed a middle class unto itself that was more about image, aspiration, values, and moral pretense than it was about economics. Bart Landry described it thus: "In the absence of class distinctions similar to those of whites, status distinctions predominated. Membership in the emerging black elite depended less on economic means or occupation than on such characteristics as family background, particularly white ancestry, skin color, and manners and morals patterned after middle class and upper class white" (Landry, 1987:28–29).

It was a class that blacks in virtually any material condition could be a part of. In this sense, the black middle class was nothing like the bourgeoisie that Karl Marx had dismissed as functionaries for the ruling class. Instead it was more like the social psychological class that Max Weber had described—a class by virtue of its own self-identification— but with very limited opportunities to express its values in enterprise and commerce in the larger society.

In 1898, W.E.B. Du Bois offered the first description of social classes among blacks, a portrait painted in part by each class's material condition, but more fully by the groups' character and public demeanor and by what Du Bois saw as family life and values (Du Bois, 1967:311):

- Class 1. Free Negroes who most often were mulattoes, had stable families, comfortable incomes, owned a home, and maintained conventional sexual behavior
- Class 2. "Respectable" people, steadily employed working-class people who had stable families, comfortable incomes, and conventional social behavior
- Class 3. The poor, who earned from comfortable to inadequate incomes, had stable to unstable households, and were not part of the "immoral or criminal elements"
- Class 4. "Vicious and criminal elements"

Du Bois was careful not to describe class 1 as "upper" and class 2 as "middle." The only distinction between class 1 and the "respectable" blacks in class 2 was social status prior to emancipation. Both classes consisted of freedmen, mulattoes, and owned property. What both classes had in common was conventional family, social, and sexual mores. This middle class emphasized legal husband-wife households as opposed to common-law marriage. Their day-to-day social lives copied those of the white upper and middle classes; they dressed, talked, and acted (in public) like the white middle class; and their homes were indistinguishable from those of the white middle class as well. This class took great pride in having a parlor in their home—"a comfortable theatre of middle class presentation" (Grier, 1988:3). The alternatives were the bright and gaudy dress of common blacks, black dialectic speech, unladylike and ungentlemanly behavior, and the dirty chaotic households of commoners.

In classes 1 and 2, men were prohibited nominally from having multiple households or having women on the side as other "wives," and respectable women had husbands devoted to them alone. These social mores were in reaction to their degrading conditions during slavery. At that time, slave masters decided whether their slaves could marry, whether a wife or husband would be sold away, and whether the master or other slaves would "lay-with"—enjoying and impregnating—young slave women. Both during and after slavery, because of extreme poverty and the high male death rate, men who were relatively well off were informally expected to support more than one household. After slavery, legal and conventional marriage and family arrangements became major status goals.

Du Bois's class 3 people were those who were without the lifestyle, family stability, and middle-class self-presentation in the "upper" classes. Lack of middle-class morals and values kept them out of class 2 even if they had the material comfort to qualify. But generally, lack of material comfort went along with lack of refinement. Class 4 was defined primarily by its "vicious" values and the expression of those values in criminal behavior. It was not that people in the lowest class were poor, unemployed, or racially oppressed; they had criminal and antisocial attitudes as well.

Du Bois's 1898 description of black classes is consistent with the peculiar circumstances of blacks under Jim Crow. No one owned or controlled "the means of production." There was no upper or ruling class. No particular occupations were identified. There was no clear distinction between people who were middling sorts and laborers. Besides a steady income and a level of comfort, the only other dividing line between classes was whether one affirmed conventional (white middle-class) social values and could act them out. In effect, there was a "middle class" only in values. Weber's Protestant ethic could exist among them; that is, one could have a very strong Protestant work ethic, but for the majority who had such a value, it was not going to increase enterprise or create capital beyond black communities. It is remarkable that Du Bois's description of black social classes was based on fieldwork he did in Philadelphia's Seventh Ward, in the urban North, rather than in the South. The majority of residents were from the South, however, and thus their community and their class system very much reflected the grip of Jim Crow. If one is tempted to dismiss Du Bois's description of class as only a status hierarchy and not the real architecture of class (Landry, 1980), another view of social stratification in black communities in the early part of the last century might supply more proof.

Such a view is found in another important descriptor of black urban social classes during the early 1900s: John Daniels's *In Freedom's Birthplace* (1914). Daniels used "upper, middle, and lower classes" in describing Boston's black social classes decades before sociologist William Lloyd Warner's popularization of these concepts. Daniels described black classes as follows:

1.   There was an upper class (2 percent of the population) consisting of mulattoes who lived in racially mixed neighborhoods and who had the highest incomes. Black- and brown-skinned Negroes of new wealth began to make slow inroads into this upper class.
2.   There was a middle class (18 percent) of Negroes who were mainly workers. They owned homes in Negro neighborhoods and had comfortable incomes.
3.   There was a lower class (70 percent) of common laborers, domestics, and personal service workers who had insufficient to comfortable incomes.
4.   There was a bottom class (10 percent) of "vicious and shiftless persons" who were most often involved in crime (Daniels, 1914:174–185).

Almost twenty years after Du Bois, Daniels described virtually the same social system as Du Bois: income, home ownership, and mulatto background were class markers. There were two differences between Daniels's and Du Bois's descriptions, however. The moral-value class dimension was less prominent in Daniels's book; he also recorded the declining monopoly of mulattoes on the highest class and status. But the major divisions between black classes still included the presence or absence of conventional morals and behaviors, and the bottom was still defined as those who were "vicious and shiftless."

One might criticize Du Bois and Daniels for their own class bias by referring to segments of the community as "vicious" and "shiftless" and by separating segments of the community based on family form and sexual morals. In retrospect, we have to consider that moral evaluations and behavioral criteria were actually used by most blacks as markers of class divisions at the turn of the last century. Du Bois and Daniels were reflecting not only their own biases but also those of their times and the views of most other blacks at that time, even though such bases of distinction may not be important in distinguishing blacks today. I have no reason to doubt that there was an objective reality reflected in Du Bois's and Daniels's descriptors. There was a social structure that severely restricted opportunity based upon race, not class. External restrictions on what blacks could and could not do for a living left noneconomic and social bases as criteria for distinction and division in black communities, such as the ones they described. By inference Du Bois and Daniels would claim that there was a large degree of overlap between class structure and the community status system.

The moral-ethical class criterion was more clearly evident in activist efforts to "uplift" the race. Literate blacks and abolition-minded whites went into the South after the Civil War on a mission to end black illiteracy and immorality, to encourage proper family life, to improve health among blacks, and to provide skills and technical training. This rehabilitative activism became even more critical during Jim Crow and was the basis of self-improvement movements in virtually every aspect of black life. For example, organized public health work began in the South in the 1870s, with black women as the primary agents of change, since it was believed that women had the most influence on the physical and moral health of their families. The National Negro Health Week was started by Booker T. Washington to popularize the need to improve health practices among blacks. The Alpha Kappa Alpha's Mississippi Health Project in 1903 was one of the first community health education outreach efforts in the nation. One of the tasks of the National Association of Colored Women was to address black women's sexual vulnerability by countering with positive "moral" images of black women (Smith, 1995). There was also the Tuskegee Movable School, which predated national cooperative extension efforts. In cooperative extension, community educators would go out to people's homes in rural areas to teach home economics and health education and to educate farmers on how to improve their crops and the productivity of their farms.

Some believed that racial segregation would end only when Negroes cleaned up their homes and moral lives (Smith, 1995). Many believed that poverty among the masses of blacks was nobody's fault but theirs and was due to their moral shortcomings; certainly Du Bois reflected this judgment in his work in Philadelphia's Seventh Ward (Gaines, 1996). By 1910, some 300,000 adults (3 percent of the black population) were formally educated. The moral-ethical dimension was so prominent at that time that education was not primarily academic. It was more vocational and moral-ethical instruction on how to live proper and "respectable" lives. Education in black institutions obligated its recipient to build up the race. This too became the basis for entry into the middle class. Converting those with "vicious" and "criminal" ways and values to "respectable" lives was much like a socioreligious mission, and some thought this was also a precondition for ending Jim Crow. But while Jim Crow lasted, living "correctly" improved one's life in spite of Jim Crow. One could at least become materially comfortable, be respected, and receive positive regard from one's family, other blacks, and fair-minded whites. To be respectable and to act respectably was also a powerful contrast to the stereotypes and racist beliefs whites held of black people.

Retrospectives studies on elite black communities reiterate Du Bois's and Daniels's observations. Such communities in Boston and Washington, D.C., lacked strong political and economic underpinnings, were ignored by the white middle and upper classes, and transformed from communities of aristocratic mulatto communities to those of educated professionals who slowly gave way to brown- and black-skinned upwardly mobile blacks (Cromwell, 1994). They emphasized "respectability," thrift, hard work, self-respect, and righteousness as family values and taught responsibility to the race (Moore, 1999). Their articulated family values were not extraordinary when compared to the family values of whites and other historical middle classes. We should remember, however, that what people proclaim as their values are not necessarily what they actually do. Their emphasis on responsibility to the race was unusual, especially when they were politically conservative and had low membership in organizations such as the NAACP, Urban League, and National Negro Business League (McBride, 1981). They also sought to live apart from and have as little day-to-day contact with the masses of blacks as possible. A critical view of their uplift ideology would suggest that their responsibility to the race had more to do with maintaining their monopoly of black customers, clients, and patients than anything else. Racial uplift that did not have them at the top of the black social hierarchy and as the only business and service providers was not supported—it was in fact fiercely opposed.

By the 1930s, others who studied black community social structure found virtually the same hierarchy as Du Bois and Daniels had. John Dollard studied black social structure in a small Mississippi city. He found a small black "upper class" consisting of professionals with good incomes who provided services to other blacks, a middle class of regularly employed and "respectable" home owners, and then the masses of blacks who were lower class (Dollard, 1937). Florence Powdermaker found virtually the same class structure in her 1930s fieldwork as had

John Daniels in 1914. Mulatto service providers were an upper class joined by nonmulatto new "wealth" (income); workers with comfortable incomes were the middle class; poorly paid common laborers and domestics were next; the "vicious" and "shiftless" were again at the bottom of the class hierarchy (Powdermaker, 1939).

Black and White Classes Contrasted

By the 1930s, the attention of social scientists turned to formal study of class in the United States. Up to this point, the term *class* had been used primarily by socialists and labor activists to rally labor in "class struggle" against the "ruling class." One-third of the labor force was unemployed during the Great Depression, another third was downwardly mobile, and socialism was at its height in the United States (Zieger, 1994). There were two major concerns of business and government leaders. The first was an empirical question: were there indeed separate and conflicting classes in the United States, and if there were, what implications did this have for the future of the nation? Second, more and more blacks were "migrating" out of the South into the large cities of the Northeast and Midwest. Were they becoming radicalized in the ghettos by exposure to socialists? Researchers in the university community were called on to get answers to these questions by studying US community life in the 1930s (Bowser, 2002).

In the late 1930s, one team headed by Yale's William Lloyd Warner moved into the small New England industrial city of Newberryport, Massachusetts, which they referred to in their research as Yankee City. They used participant observation, a social anthropological technique, to systematically interview residents. They started at the two obvious extremes: the well-off industrialists at the top, and the poorest of the city's workers at the bottom. They asked respondents several questions: Who were the peers with whom they socialized? Who were they better off than? With whom did they not socialize? Who were the people who were worse off, so that they did not want to socialize with them? The researchers worked through social affiliations from the top and bottom of the community, mapping out social networks until their teams met in the middle. William Lloyd Warner was quoted as describing the divisions they found, or "social classes," as follows:

> By class is meant two or more orders of people who are believed to be and are accordingly ranked by the members of the community in socially superior and inferior positions. . . . To belong to a particular

level in the social-class system of America means that a family or individual has gained acceptance as an equal by those who belong in the class. The behavior in this class and the participation of those in it must be rated by the rest of the community as being at a particular place in the social scale. (Warner quoted in Gordon, 1963:89–90)

Their work revealed a sixfold hierarchy in Yankee City whose terms have become part of contemporary conventional language, but whose origins in research are obscure to the general public (Warner and Lunt, 1941:91). The hierarchy is as follows:

The Class of Inherited Wealth
- Upper-upper class: Families who had maintained inherited wealth across multiple generations and who were the primary investors and owners of industry, property, and financial institutions
- Lower-upper class: Families in their second generation of inherited wealth and junior partners relative to old-line families in investments and ownership

The Class of Achievement
- Upper-middle class: Individuals who had attained affluence and recognition as leaders in their professions and as managers, directors, and heads of industry, financial institutions, colleges and universities, churches, and so on
- Lower-middle class: Entry-level professionals in strategic fields such as law, business, medicine, accounting, banking, and so on; professionals in service fields such as teachers, librarians, nurses, and social workers; and higher-skilled craftspersons and technicians

The Class of the "Common Man"
- Upper-lower class: Regularly employed and well-compensated union laborers, supervisors, and technical workers
- Lower-lower class: Irregularly employed and poorly compensated workers who were generally not unionized

Critics assert that Warner and his team intentionally created an alternative to the Marxist class perspective. Defenders respond that the Marxist view was simply not empirically correct. Research conducted in a midwestern city in 1924, prior to Warner's research, found virtually the same social divisions that Warner had found (Lynd and Lynd, 1929). The major difference was that Robert and Helen Lynd did not explicitly use the class concept. In their 1930s follow-up fieldwork, they found that the old upper-class families had sold their plants or converted them to corporations, had taken less visible roles as major investors, and were now pleased to have new corporate managers become the new focus of public scorn (Lynd and Lynd, 1937).

Warner's social class model initially was not intended to reflect social class among blacks, but it was adapted by St. Clair Drake and Horace Cayton, who did participant observation in Chicago's Southside as part of their doctoral training at the University of Chicago. As shown in Figure 4.1, the result was the first and most comprehensive model of black social classes based upon Warner's model (Drake and Cayton, 1945).

The Drake and Cayton social class hierarchy is divided into Warner's three main social class divisions—upper, middle, and lower.

Figure 4.1   The System of Social Classes in Bronzeville

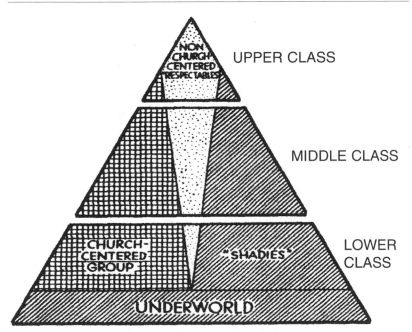

Source: Figure from S. C. Drake and H. Cayton, *Black Metropolis: A Study of Negro Life in a Northern City* (New York: Harcourt, Brace and Company, 1945), p. 525, copyright 1945 by St. Claire Drake and Horace R. Cayton and renewed 1973 by St. Claire Drake and Susan Woodson, reprinted by permission of Harcourt, Inc.

But within each black social class there is an additional (vertical) division based upon separate constellations of values, worldview, and extralegal occupations. Drake and Cayton described them as follows:

> The class structure in Bronzeville is not a simple tripartite system through which individuals move by attaining the class-behavior pattern which their occupational and educational position permits and their training stimulates. Within each class there is a group, proportionately smallest in the upper class and largest in the lower class, which has secured and maintained its position by earning its income in pursuits not generally recognized by the community as "respectable." (Drake and Cayton, 1945:524)

The people who made their livings in nonrespectable pursuits were referred to as "shady" and were part of the racketeer hierarchy. In the Chicago of the 1930s, gambling, bootlegging alcohol (before the end of Prohibition), "policy" (a community lottery), late-night clubs, and prostitution were ways to make a living in the face of massive unemployment. Drake and Cayton recognized that there were members of the black community in each economic level whose source of income was from the rackets. There also was a parallel church-related hierarchy whose primary values and worldview were religious and whose social affiliations were built around church membership. In this church-related class sector, people and churches were divided by social class based on income and property ownership or lack of it. The orientation in the center of Figure 4.1 is of nonchurch "respectables" (race leaders and club society). This group became proportionately larger as one went up the class hierarchy. These people affirmed the centrality of economic means as definitive in their lives and of political institutions as the basis of change. As people in the church-affiliated world rejected a purely secular or economic worldview as "ungodly," secularists rejected the purely religious view as backward and retreatist. These extraeconomic divisions are more fully elaborated extensions into the 1930s of the moral-ethic division reported by Du Bois and Daniels earlier in the century.

Comparing Class by Race

When we compare Warner's social class model with Drake and Cayton's, there are some obvious differences in black and white social classes. Both models have upper classes, but Drake and Cayton's upper class is nothing like Warner's. In black Chicago, the upper class did not consist of families with intergenerational inherited wealth (as opposed to income) sufficient for them to live off of the interest. Black "upper-class" families did not own or manage the major businesses in Chicago, nor were they the most politically influential. The black "upper class," if looked at as part of Warner's system, was at best an upper middle class of top achievers from the church, secular-respectable (race leaders and clubs), and racketeer hierarchies—top-paid preachers and ministers, businessmen and professionals, and leaders of organized crime. If they had been in a white community, they would *not* have been upper class. Drake and Cayton's middle class consisted of regularly employed and comfortable residents who were the equivalent of Warner's lower-middle class. In effect, the equivalent social classes among blacks were at least one level below those among whites.

When we look back from Drake and Cayton to Du Bois and Daniels, we can also see how black social class structure changed from the post-Reconstruction period to the eve of World War II. Mulatto birth gave way to professional achievement and income as the foundation for highest standing in black communities. The very strong moral-ethical basis for class standing at the turn of 1900 gave way to competing value hierarchies—church, secular, and rackets—if they were not there to begin with. The old "vicious" and criminal underclass that Du Bois and Daniels wrote of continued in the 1930s as an "underworld" at the bottom of the lower class. But the most important insight to be drawn from these studies is the difference in social class between black and white communities. By 1945 it was clearly recognized that there were different social class systems in white and black communities. Figure 4.2 graphically shows the main difference between Warner and Drake and Cayton.

Again, there is no equivalent of the white upper class among blacks, so that the top black class is the equivalent of the second-highest white class and so on. Jim Crow segregation and restrictions prohibited blacks from generating wealth across generations that could increase in value and be protected and augmented through political influence. The high-achieving members of the black Jim Crow middle class caused confusion, so that they were sometimes regarded as an upper class because there were no other blacks above them. Blacks constituted a subordinate and separate social class hierarchy within the larger white class system. The line between black and white hierarchies constituted a uniquely US caste system, despite criticism of the caste concept (Cox, 1948). This meant that blacks, by virtue of ascribed

Figure 4.2   Black and White Classes Compared

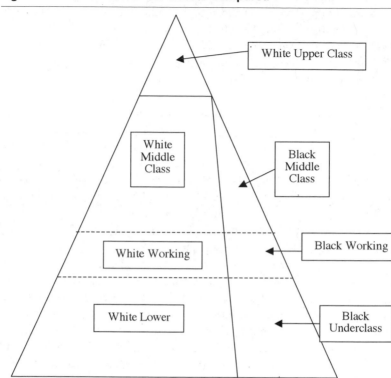

African ancestry, could not enter the larger social hierarchy defined by European ancestry under the banner of "whiteness."

By 1940, the new Jim Crow black middle class had attained a milestone, despite racial segregation and despite violence and lynchings aimed at destroying black aspirations and economic challenges to whites. This class had achieved greater longevity than the Reconstruction middle class. By the time Drake and Cayton's study was published in 1945, the Jim Crow black middle class was well into its second generation.

In Retrospect

Jim Crow was never simply about separating whites from blacks. It was about making certain that blacks never realized their full political and economic potential as they had threatened to do during Black Reconstruction. If blacks had not been restricted, they would have politically dominated minority white populations in several southern states and in numerous counties in other states. They would have been a powerful force throughout the region and the nation. One of the by-products of Jim Crow was the diminishing of black social classes in comparison to whites. A second by-product was that the organization or structure of black social classes that developed under Jim Crow was sufficiently different that neither of the classic notions of class described by Marx and Weber fit. This is particularly the case with the black middle class. Blacks were labor in the South and were the most accessible labor force for new northern industries after the Civil War. Any labor struggle after 1865 would also have been more decisive with blacks as prominent members of the proletariat. But instead they were passed over for European immigrants.

The fact is that William Lloyd Warner did not disprove Marx and affirm Weber for whites, nor did Drake and Cayton do the same for blacks. Warner set out to provide an alternative to Marx and found social classes instead of a Marxist proletariat in conflict with a ruling class. Warner's method precluded investigating whether there was class consciousness and conflict between the top and bottom of the social order. If such classes and conflict existed, he would not have found them with the methods he used. But this does not mean that a Marxist class structure did not exist in the 1930s. There is considerable evidence from other sources that the 1930s and the Great Depression was the time when US capitalism was most threatened by radical labor (Foner, 1962). Indeed, the reforms undertaken by the administration of Franklin Roosevelt, which now constitute the most basic of contemporary US entitlements, were all advocated by socialist labor and instituted by the federal government to co-opt labor's anticapitalist momentum: Social Security, the five-day and forty-hour workweek, unemployment insurance, workplace safety, public housing, and aid for dependent children (now eliminated) (Piven and Cloward, 1993: 60–61, 76–77). The point is: Warner's social classes do not preclude Marxist classes.

In contrast, Drake and Cayton were not in a position to question Warner's model. After all, they were Ph.D. students and were following their advisers' methods. But they still managed to provide a unique contribution and not only about black classes. They provided an insight that reflects back on the larger white society. The vertical divisions of social class (church, secular, and shady) like the ones that Drake and Cayton found in black Chicago probably existed among European immigrants as well, before these groups fully conformed to Anglo-American expectations and were assimilated into the US middle class. The extent to which these vertical divisions impact classes, as Max Weber and Karl Marx defined them, is still unknown.

Vertical divisions of social class enable us to build noneconomic distinctions into the concept of class stratification. This allows us to make the following assumptions with regard to Max Weber's notions of the Protestant ethic: A community can believe strongly in and act out a "Protestant (work) ethic" as best it can, but these efforts can be either disproportionately rewarded or frustrated because of noneconomic factors. As such, these other (vertical) social factors, as Weber suggested, may in fact be as important as one's income and relations to the means of production. In the United States in the 1800s and the first half of the 1900s, these extraeconomic factors were race, ethnicity, and religion (Blumin, 1989). Having the right job and material comfort were not sufficient to determine one's class standing: one also had to have the right identity in these other social divisions—preferably one would be male, Protestant, white, and of English ancestry. The black experience in producing and sustaining a middle class speaks to the importance of race in the United States as a factor in determining one's position in social class hierarchy.

The same applies to Marx's perspective. All that is important to ideological Marxism is a dialectic and conflicting relationship between the ruling class who owns the means of production and the working class whose labor is exploited. Drake and Cayton's model suggested that vertical noneconomic divisions not only exist between people in the same economic class but that these other divisions can restrain conflict between people in the same and in different classes. Both the church and racketeer hierarchies restrained the ability of secular "race leaders," who might have had a Marxist view, to mobilize blacks around class and racial injustices and to act politically. Those in the church-related hierarchy considered economic injustice to be unimportant and even the will of God, to be tolerated in this lifetime because there is no such injustice in the next world. The crime-related hierarchy could not act politically because they operated illegally and had to remain as anonymous as possible. In effect, any attempt at Marxist class action had to overcome the influence of two other worlds (church and criminal).

Who was the black lower class or proletariat to struggle against? The black "upper class" controlled little of importance, did not employ the majority of blacks, and was certainly not a "ruling class." Blacks, and by extension other ethnic groups, could struggle all they wanted within their own class hierarchy, but in so doing would change very little about inequality in the larger society. To access real power and the real ruling class, blacks would have had to cut across the racial caste line to challenge the white upper class. If they had chosen to do this, however, their actions simply would have been criminalized and condemned as racial rather than part of some class struggle. So when blacks rioted in Harlem in 1935 over poor jobs and unemployment, it was called a "race riot" and not workers striking out against capitalists (Baritz, 1989). Marx would have been shocked to see white workers opposing blacks because their white racial status was threatened and because race was more important than a common class identity and interests. Both Weber's and Marx's classic notions of class were based on homogeneous societies in which ethnic, racial, and religious divisions were less important than economic distinctions.

The next chapter sets the stage for the emergence of yet a third black middle class and explores why it became so important to obscure the structural differences between black and white social classes in the present.

5

Comparability
. . . Not

For the first half of the 1900s, the black middle class hardly grew in size because of the persistent opposition of southern whites against black progress. If we take white-collar work as an approximate measure of the size of the black middle class, then it was estimated that in 1910 only 3 percent of black workers more than fourteen years of age held white-collar jobs compared to 24 percent of whites (Landry, 1987). By 1940, it was possible to better identify white-collar work in the decennial census as professional, technical, managerial, and supervisory work. Table 5.1 shows the growth in the number and percentage of blacks who had access to middle-class income and jobs and who could claim middle-class status by virtue of their work and income in comparison to their white peers between 1940 and 1970.

Between 1910 and 1940, the proportion of black labor that did white-collar work nationally increased by only 1 percent. From 1940 through 1960, the proportion of blacks doing white-collar work increased as a proportion of black workers from 4 percent in 1940 to 7 percent by 1960. In those twenty years, the percentage of blacks doing white-collar work almost doubled growing at more than three times the rate of the prior thirty years. This rapid growth occurred prior to changes brought about by the post–World War II civil rights movement. At this rate of growth, was affirmative action even necessary? There is an answer to this question as well as an explanation.

Table 5.1   Number (in thousands) and Percentage of Black and White Employed Workers 14 Years and Over Who Did White-Collar Work and Their Ratio, 1910–1970

	Employed Blacks	% Blacks Employed as White-Collar Workers	Employed Whites	% Whites Employed as White-Collar Workers	Black/White Ratio
1910		3		24	.13
1940	4,479	4	40,495	17	.23
1960	6,097	7	58,010	21	.33
1970	420	10	68,972	23	.43

Source: 1910 statistics are from B. Landry, *The New Black Middle Class* (Berkeley: University of California Press, 1987); 1940 to 1970 statistics are from US Census Bureau, *The Social and Economic Status of the Black Population in the United States, 1790–1978,* vol. series P-23, no. 80 (Washington, D.C.: US Government Printing Office, 1979), p. 74.

Note: Statistics on white-collar workers in Table 5.1 do not include sales, clerical, and kindred workers in order to be roughly comparable to management, professional, and related occupations in the 2000 Census.

The Impact of World War II and Migration

The growth of the black middle class between World War II and the civil rights legislation of the 1960s could be explained in part by two factors—the need for labor created by World War II and the accelerated migration of blacks out of the South after the war.

World War II curtailed the flow of European immigrants to the United States at the same time that millions of young white men were drafted into the military. Both of these developments produced an unprecedented demand for labor. Winning the war was as much dependent upon the rapid production of ships, trucks, weapons, uniforms, and so on at home as it was on military success in Europe and the Pacific. In order to access the labor supply on the home front to win the war, it was necessary to temporarily overlook prewar social norms. Despite continued racial discrimination, African Americans were hired for skilled and well-paying jobs that ordinarily would have been reserved for white men (Wynn, 1976). Blacks gladly fled the South in large numbers to fill these jobs in the Northeast, Midwest, and West.

Flight from the South was not new. A generation had done just that before the war. What was different after 1940 was the scale of the departure. Between 1940 and 1960, blacks declined from 43 percent to 35 percent of the population in South Carolina, from 35 percent to 28 percent of the population in Georgia, and from 49 percent to 42 percent in Mississippi. Blacks increased from 5 percent to 10 percent of the population in Illinois, from 4 percent to 8 percent in New York, and from 2 percent to 6 percent in California (US Census Bureau, 1979). When the war ended, white men returned to their well-paying jobs, but the industrial sector that had hired blacks continued to expand and to employ them. By 1960, black migration and the entry of blacks in large numbers into industrial work had led to the formation of even larger urban black working-class communities in Philadelphia, New York, Boston, Pittsburgh, Chicago, St. Louis, Los Angeles, and other cities. It was this rapid expansion of black working-class communities and industrial employment that created opportunities for the expansion of the black service (Jim Crow) middle class prior to affirmative action.

Getting out of the South and into the industrial economy more than doubled the number of blacks doing white-collar work, which roughly doubled the size of the black middle class in twenty years (Fligstein, 1981). Then between 1960 and 1970, the proportion of blacks who did white-collar work increased again, this time from 7 percent to 10 percent. This growth rate in one decade was double the unprecedented growth of the prior two decades (1940 to 1960). But migration from the South is not a sufficient explanation for black middle-class growth in the 1960s, because by 1970 black migration from the South had virtually ended, as had black industrialization (Jaynes and Williams, 1989).

The continued growth of the black middle class after 1960 was due to the enforcement of new civil rights laws, racial desegregation, and federal affirmative action. Let us assume that migration and the repositioning of substantial numbers of African Americans outside the South in the 1960s continued to fuel the growth of blacks in white-collar jobs at the same rate that it had from 1940. If this is true, then half of the growth in black white-collar workers (and the middle class) during the 1960s could be attributed to the decade's civil rights initiatives to end Jim Crow and racial discrimination nationally. But this change attributed to the civil rights movement did not just happen; a particular set of circumstances led to the movement's success. It is worth reviewing these circumstances to better understand how the black middle class grew so rapidly at this time and so thoroughly transformed itself after 1960.

The End of Jim Crow

World War II was fought against the Nazi and Japanese fascist beliefs about racial supremacy. In order to convince the US public to support the war, the federal government and press had to produce ideological critiques of German and Japanese fascism and racism that inadvertently applied to US Jim Crow as well (Finkle, 1975; Savage, 2003). The parallels between a racist Nazi Germany and a racist Jim Crow South were obvious even to casual observers. The idea that the world could be against one and ignore the other was not lost on even the most ardent racists. By the end of the war in 1945, it was only a matter of time before Jim Crow would have to be addressed.

World War II did something else. It put more than a million Africans, Asians, and African Americans under arms to fight against German, Italian, and Japanese fascism (Wynn, 1976). Men who had been consigned to an inferior status before the war were now being asked to kill white and Japanese men, the allegedly superior races. Black troops from the United States and Africa who were armed and had fought had a very different disposition toward racial subordination by the time they returned home (Dalfiume, 1969; Wynn, 1971). There was no way the former African colonies could return to business as usual under European colonial masters. Rising expectations throughout the world after the war would end direct European colonialism. Nationalist movements in every former colony emerged stronger after the war and demanded independence for the same reasons World War II had been fought. At home, African American war veterans returned from fighting Germans and made it very clear that they would no longer tolerate Jim Crow.

The Spark

Jim Crow was ripe for challenge, with worldwide rising expectations for change among people of color and a large and dispersed black working class in the United States. The 1954 Supreme Court decision *Brown v. Board of Education* outlawed racial segregation in schools and signaled the legal end of the 1896 *Plessy v. Ferguson* doctrine. "Separate but equal" as the pillar of Jim Crow laws and practices was finally judged to be what it had been all along—unequal and racially oppressive. But it was the Montgomery, Alabama, bus boycott begun in 1956 that lit a fire to Jim Crow (Branch, 1989). The bus boycott was targeted at the indignity of blacks' having to give up their seats to whites and move to the back of city buses. It is no coincidence that this boycott was urban based and started out of working-class necessity—to get to and from work. All African Americans who had experienced Jim Crow experienced this indignity and could come together nationally to support this boycott.

This was not the first time blacks had challenged Jim Crow. There was opposition all during the first half of the 1900s. There were labor boycotts, small demonstrations in southern cities, and silent protests at black colleges during the 1920s (Morris, 1999). White businesses in northern and midwestern black communities that would not hire blacks were effectively boycotted before 1940. Martin Luther King Sr. led protest demonstrations in Atlanta during the 1930s. There were also small groups that worked for social change in the South. The Joint Committee on Race Relations of the Society of Friends (Quakers) sponsored a Peace Caravan through the South in 1932 to collect signatures for the First World Disarmament Conference in Geneva (Bowser, 2002). Their Fellowship of Reconciliation used Mohandas Gandhi's nonviolent tactics in the South in antiwar and antiracist projects long before Martin Luther King Jr. adopted these methods. The NAACP prior to 1940 was a radical organization with members and field offices throughout the South. Even the Communist Party sent speakers and organizers into the South to work against peonage—sharecropping. The party was instrumental in popularizing the 1934 Georgia case of Angelo Herndon, a young black man scheduled to be executed for a questionable offense under an 1860 slave insurrection law that was still in effect (Kelley, 1990; Martin, 1976).

Given the history of protests in the South during Jim Crow, it was not extraordinary that the Montgomery bus boycott occurred and was led by a young black minister. The difference in 1954 from prior efforts was the timing of the boycott and the other interests prepared to capitalize on it. If the boycott had occurred before World War II, it most likely would have been a short protest rather than an outright boycott. It is also unlikely that it would have succeeded, and it certainly would not have expanded beyond Montgomery, Alabama, to become a national movement. But by 1953, there was a sizable national black working class able to materially and morally support the boycott, and there was a "civil rights" movement. National retailers such as Woolworth Department Stores with segregated stores in the South now could be pressured to desegregate by a national boycott. Black working-class retail spending was sizable enough that white businesses throughout the nation and urban South had become heavily dependent on these dollars. Blacks now could bring economic pressure to bear on white politicians and the business community that could not have been imagined in 1910.

In addition, the considerable experience of the Quaker Fellowship of Reconciliation in conducting nonviolent protest was at King's disposal through Bayard Ruston, who linked King with postwar antiracist interests among US labor unions and churches (D'Emilio, 2003). All the ingredients were present to make the Montgomery bus boycott not only a success in its own right but also the spark igniting a national movement. But even these resources and prospects were insufficient to collapse sixty years of Jim Crow. Two additional significant factors contributed to the erosion: television coverage and international attention.

Television. Television brought the boycott, the protests, the marches, and the violent reactions of white southerners and state authorities against the movement into the nation's living rooms as nothing else could have (Graham, 2003). The beatings of nonviolent black and white demonstrators, the hatred against blacks, and the formal system of racial segregation had gone on as long as it had in part because it had been isolated in the South. The visual images of white violence and hatred offended national middle-class sensibilities. Many were shocked to see separate white and "colored" entrances to buildings and even separate water fountains. To southern whites, African Americans were a nameless, hateful presence referred to only through epithets.

Television was also used by the Congress of Racial Equality (CORE), which had formerly been the Fellowship of Reconciliation. It had been conducting the same nonviolent protests for years, but before television little attention was paid to them. In the new civil rights protests, black and white protesters sat in the front seats of interstate buses and refused to move to the rear when they entered the South. This was in absolute defiance of Jim Crow. The violence of police and white mobs against these riders was captured on television and broadcast all across the country and throughout the world.

An international issue. International attention was the second critical factor essential to forcing the passage of the 1964 Civil Rights Act, which outlawed racial segregation in the nation and produced the presidential executive order for affirmative action. For more than sixty years the federal government had ignored racial segregation, the lynching of blacks, and racial violence in the South against blacks. Southern senators and representatives, who at the time were all Democrats, were a very powerful group in Congress and blocked any congressional attention to Jim Crow. J. Edger Hoover, director of the Federal Bureau of Investigation (FBI), opposed investigating civil rights violations against blacks. Lyndon Johnson, coming into the presidency after the assassination of John Kennedy, did not have strong interests in civil rights or a desire to dismantle Jim Crow. He did not particularly care for Martin Luther King Jr., who was seen as an agitator forcing Johnson and the nation to address an unpopular issue (Caro, 1990). There was no political capital at home in the South for the president to champion black civil rights. He could not win popular support in the South regardless of what he did. Even in the middle of the protests, televised beatings of demonstrators, and police dog attacks on blacks, proposed civil rights legislation could not have survived in Congress, let alone been enacted into law without an additional push.

One thing was different at this point. Unlike any other time in the 1900s, the federal government was concerned with the image of the United States in the eyes of the third world. The United States and Western Europe were competing with the socialist second world of the Soviet Union and China for influence in the third world (Plummer, 2003). Why? Whoever got access to the third world's natural resources, labor, and strategic locations had a decisive long-term advantage over the other, just as had been the case in the colonial period. With which side would these newly independent nations and former colonies in Africa and Asia align themselves? The West had its colonial past as a clear strike against it. But the United States had a special vulnerability—Jim Crow. How could the United States claim to be the leader of the "free world," a model of democracy and of progressive capitalism against socialism, when it maintained racial segregation in the South? If Jim Crow could have been ignored and its domestic opposition silenced, then US propaganda might have worked. But US hypocrisy would have been too obvious. Civil rights protests were being telecast for people all over the world to see.

The Soviets and Chinese were most eager to show the events in the South to the third world. If white Americans treated African Americans that way, did it not seem that white Americans would consider Africans and Asians inferior as well? In addition, one did not have to rely simply on communist propaganda about the "real" United States. Diplomats from the newly independent African nations came to Washington, D.C., a segregated southern city, where they too were discriminated against and experienced Jim Crow firsthand. There was no way the United States could win the hearts and minds of the third world and then have access to all its resources while a Jim Crow South still existed and while the attention of the nation and world was on the protests and demonstrations against it.

The federal government could no longer defend Jim Crow or continue to ignore it because of the strategic interests of the nation (Dudziak, 2000). President Kennedy's and then President Johnson's leadership in passing the 1964 Civil Rights Act, essentially outlawing racial segregation, was not done simply out of high moral sentiment or because of Martin Luther King Jr. Jim Crow was outlawed in the national interest. In effect, the US government was embarrassed into ridding itself of the system of racial oppression modeled by Nazi Germany and Apartheid South Africa. In doing so, the underlying restraints against the expansion of the black middle class were removed. But there were additional pressure points for civil rights.

The Fire Next Time

The expanded black working class that came out of World War II was in trouble literally from the moment it developed. What few understood at the time was that manufacturing and labor-intensive industries in US cities were in decline (Bluestone and Harrison, 1982). All during the 1950s, as African Americans celebrated their good fortune and expected more, their newly established job base was sliding out from under them. It was being moved overseas to Asia and Latin America. Also, entry-level industrial work that remained in the United States was being automated and moved to suburban and rural locations along the new interstate highway system. The bottom line was that blacks had inherited obsolete jobs in declining industries. It was the same case in housing; blacks got the oldest and least desirable housing in the oldest, least desirable cities. In the 1950s, the new jobs seemed better paying and the housing seemed better only in comparison to what had been left behind in the South. But by the early 1960s, the underlying reality became apparent. The number of African Americans in industrial cities was steadily rising, but entry-level jobs were steadily declining.

Rising expectations and new personal freedoms met unemployment and "the ghetto" head-on. Ghettoization (segregating a people in a designated residential area through housing discrimination), police brutality, and informal racial discrimination in employment, health care, and education were the new faces of Jim Crow. The result was black rather than white urban riots on a national scale for the first time in US history. The riots did not occur in one or two cities: more than 200 occurred all across the country from 1963 to 1970 (Kerner et al., 1968).

They were violent, long, and costly. The most violent ones were beyond the capacity of even the National Guard to control and required regular army units to put them down. All of this was also televised worldwide and constituted a second blow to US credibility in its competition with the socialist world.

The riots occurred at the same time that there was growing discontent among civil rights workers in the South over what the civil rights movement's goals should be. They began to recognize that civil rights did not address the political and economic inequities of racism. The end result of civil rights efforts was that blacks could now sit at any lunch counter in the South and buy a hamburger, but one might not be able to afford the hamburger and certainly could not buy the restaurant. Discontent with political and economic progress among civil rights workers and blacks in general had already led to a call by Kwame Ture (Stokely Carmichael) for "black power." Malcolm X left the inward-looking Nation of Islam and made intellectual and ideological connections between the plight of "Africans in America" and people of color throughout the world. Then Martin Luther King Jr. became a Noble Peace Laureate and made it clear that he was not going to stop with civil rights. He saw the next phase of the movement as human and economic rights. In addition, he came out against the war in Vietnam.

The growing black potential to destabilize (white) elite domestic and foreign agendas was simply too great to ignore. Former President Dwight Eisenhower was one of the first to warn that the United States had developed an industrial and military power elite, a point amplified by C. Wright Mills (1957). This elite's worst fear in the 1960s was that the thousands of black urban rioters would come together around human rights focused on domestic economic inequities, would respond to a call for black power "by any means necessary," and would align themselves with foreign anticolonial efforts. Then there was the nightmare that King and Malcolm X might align blacks with the already troublesome and growing movement against the Vietnam War. These possibilities could not be ignored and certainly not in the midst of a Cold War with the socialist world and a hotly contested war in Vietnam. Something had to be done and fast.

Response to Unrest

Besides the Civil Rights Act, President Johnson and Congress passed a series of antipoverty and job training bills aimed at alienated urban blacks. Suddenly, there was job training, money for education, a food program, child care, more aid for dependent children, and new public housing. That was the easy part. The hard part came when Johnson, in September 1965, also ordered a provision that would not have passed through Congress even in the 1960s, Executive Order No. 11246. It called for all federal agencies, all employers that did business with the federal government, and all organizations receiving federal funds to act "affirmatively" to hire blacks whenever possible. Critics warned that antipoverty measures and affirmative action were attempts to deflect black discontent and militancy and to divert attention from racially motivated political and economic inequities (Piven and Cloward, 1993).

Just in case government antipoverty and affirmative action measures did not work to reduce riots and black militancy, there was a second and hidden agenda. Several federal agencies launched Counter Intelligence Program (COINTELPRO) operations to disrupt, discredit, jail, and otherwise silence civil rights and black nationalist organizations and leaders (Churchill and Vander Wall, 1990). It did not matter that government-sponsored disruption, misinformation, and police assassinations were illegal and unconstitutional. Even though the existence of COINTELPRO has been disclosed, there have never been congressional hearings, lawsuits, or investigations of the extent and impact of US government disruption of noncriminal organizations or of the practice of discrediting and assassinating individuals because of their political and social views. It seems likely to be more than a coincidence that the two leaders who could have joined black urban militancy with the human rights and antiwar movements were both assassinated: Malcolm X in 1964 and Martin Luther King Jr. in 1968 (Churchill and Vander Wall, 1990). Out of these events came a continued decline in black urban communities, the end of civil rights and black power militancy, and, ironically, the emergence of a new black middle class.

Sudden Comparability

Prior to 1940, social scientists had been aware that Jim Crow had led to the formation of a distinct and severely restricted social class system among blacks. The prewar classic studies of US communities in the South and in the urban North had provided detailed evidence of the differences between blacks and whites in the same social class (see discussion in Chapter 4). But by 1970, these differences in black and white social classes were gone. One has to ask, did the differences really disappear with the passage of the 1964 Civil Rights Acts and with racial desegregation in US society, or were racial class differences simply ignored? To answer this question, we need to look carefully at how racial class differences were addressed in the 1960s and early 1970s. One post–civil rights change was the obscuring of social class differences within and between races.

Obscuring Class Differences

Prosperity and Consumerism

The first thing to obscure racial class differences was the post–World War II prosperity, which triggered a wave of consumerism unseen at any other time in the twentieth century. Despite differences in income, wealth, and background, black and white working- and middle-class Americans could buy the same clothes, cars, and household appliances and could amuse themselves in much the same way (Hurley, 2001). Despite their substantial differences, they began to look materially alike in public. This blurring of publicly visible differences did not occur only between the races; by 1960 the white working class had sufficient income and consumer power to really think of itself as middle class (Zunz, Schoppa, and Hiwatari, 2002). In a consumer-based society, no one was going to tell members of the working class otherwise. It was important for them to believe they had reached the American dream. The general sense of US social class can be put into context when we consider that by 1930, many working-class white Americans began to see themselves as "middle class" long before they had middle-class income, education, or work (Baritz, 1989).

The Legacy of World War II

The second development that clouded class differences resulted from the World War II victory over fascism. The war was a triumph of bureaucratic organization and management and a cloaking of the mainstream upper class. Prior to the Great Depression, there were stark reminders of social class differences in US society. Factories, in fact entire industries, were owned by very celebrated individuals with well-known names such as Carnegie, Rockefeller, and Vanderbilt. Their wealth and power could not be ignored; their very persons were daily reminders of what Marxist and non-Marxist alike called the "upper" or "ruling" class. In their landmark study, Robert and Helen Lynd observed the changing face of this "upper" class and described how these individuals controlled big business in the transition of "middle towns" between 1914 and 1934 (Lynd and

Lynd, 1929; 1937). The renowned owners of big businesses in Middletown had sold their companies or converted them to corporations by the time of the Lynds' follow-up study. It appeared as if these extraordinarily wealthy and famous individuals were ebbing as a class into the nation's middle class. In fact, the wealthy were finding ways to evade close public scrutiny and to elude labor opposition; they embedded themselves as major shareholders and "controlling interests" in now publicly owned corporations. A new class of professional managers rose in their place to run their corporations and to become the new object of public contempt. By the end of World War II, the obscuring of the upper class was virtually complete. Corporate boards and their managers ran corporations, and the controlling influence of the upper class was carefully camouflaged.

Likewise, small-business owners were very important symbols of middle-class life at the start of the twentieth century. Unlike members of the upper class, small-business owners made themselves very accessible, since their work required contact with the public. Virtually every consumer need was met by this group. As a class, they initially were better off materially than most of their customers. But people did not resent them for it. They saw that local merchants and professionals were not wealthy and did not control business like big industrialists. They were, however, clearly part of the middle sector. With post–World War II consumerism, the differences among customers, owners of small businesses, and professionals were not obvious.

Part of the disappearance of small-business owners as middle-class models has to do with a decline in the centrality and profitability of urban small businesses. This was the result of the growth of franchise outlets, national chain stores, and international mega-retail corporations (Braverman, 1974; Phillips, 1993). As a result, local retail merchants have slid down the class hierarchy and have stopped serving as daily reminders of middle-class status and prosperity.

The Role of the Social Sciences

The third development that obscured the differences between classes and races occurred in the social sciences. As World War II approached, there was mounting criticism of the qualitative methods used to study US community life. Some social scientists had serious reservations about the extent to which conclusions based upon community observation and interview studies could be generalized to other communities (House, 1934). William Lloyd Warner's Yankee City studies had developed the most extensive notion of social class and status divisions in the prewar period. The Yankee City descriptions of social class also became the most well known to the general public. Today we still use Warner's terminology of "upper class" and "middle class." As pointed out in Chapter 4, Warner's work was also the model for the most extensive study of class and status among African Americans, namely, Drake and Cayton's *Black Metropolis*. Critiques of Warner's model of social class, some of which predate his work, are as follows:

1. Status groups (such as the working and middle classes) may not be real social entities, having separate existences from one another. They may be instead a continuum without discrete points (Gross, 1908).
2. Everyone in a community may not see status divisions in totality or as discrete social classes. Social classes may be only the researcher's construction (Chinoy, 1950).
3. Classes as status groupings ignore the primary role of economic forces in social stratification. The key role of the economy and stratification of work is replaced by status groupings that are in fact only outcomes of economic organization (Mills, 1942).
4. Warner could have constructed a classification more consistent with his respondents' evaluation of status levels than he did (Gordon, 1949).
5. The Yankee City research failed to show dynamic relationships consisting of the interplay of economic status positions over a number of generations. In effect, one cannot fully see status or stratification dynamics over the course of a single generation (Merton, 1952).
6. For a classification (such as Warner's social classes) of such importance, very little attention was given to political or community power organizations.

These critiques fall into two categories. Some question the validity of Warner's class status construct, and others charge that Warner's construct did not capture all of the important dimensions of class in community life. By the beginning of World War II, there was great interest in finding ways to address questions of validity in social research and of incorporating missing dimensions into the notion of social class.

The desire to advance social research during World War II accelerated the shift from qualitative community studies to quantitative research. The War Department used social scientists extensively to study troop selection and morale and to gather public opinion regarding the war (Stouffer et al., 1949a, 1949b). Strategic and practical questions needed quick and accurate answers. Therefore, sampling theory, survey methods, and the use of statistics advanced rapidly. After the war, social scientists were enthused that these tools could significantly improve social scientific knowledge. By applying these methods to general society, there could be a vast improvement in the validity and reliability of knowledge over the qualitative approaches used prior to the war. Regional survey research centers were set up. Federal and foundation money shifted funding to more rigorous research methods, and a new generation of social scientists conducted survey research as opposed to ethnographic fieldwork.

One of the first things that social scientists wanted to do was test the validity of prewar notions of social class—to revisit the Warner descriptions of social class. But first, it was necessary to convert qualitative descriptors of social class into quantifiable factors in order to measure social class differences. Of all the descriptive details derived from the Warner studies, only two were immediately quantifiable—years of education and income. The other qualitative descriptors of social class were either not readily quantifiable or could not be derived easily or directly. These descriptors included (class) values, occupational status, family economic circumstances, family job contacts and knowledge, ability to exercise influence over political authorities, acquisition of financial resources other than income (wealth), and inheritance of family wealth or poverty. Unfortunately, racial differences in prewar communities, in addition to social class differences, were more evident in all of the qualitative factors other than income and education. By 1950, the stage was set for comparisons of black and white middle classes without regard to their prewar class differences.

The Road to Racial Class Comparability

In the 1960s, the need to eliminate racial discrimination in education, government services, employment, and public accommodations (retail trade, travel, and access in all public places) created a new requirement: the need to measure the extent to which racial inequality existed and could be eliminated in US life. Southern whites and, in particular, their congressmen defended Jim Crow and opposed civil rights; they were the first to claim that the Civil Rights Acts and affirmative action were unfair to whites. In contrast, the elimination of racial segregation was not moving fast enough for blacks. They believed more could be done to eradicate economic discrimination and inequality.

The Kennedy and Johnson presidential administrations had to show the world community that racial progress was being made in the United States. Measuring inequality, and then showing progress toward eliminating it, became a centrally important activity. After 1965, the research journals and the national press were full of articles comparing black and white Americans on almost every basis imaginable. In these articles, income and education quickly became the established measures of socioeconomic status and position and measurement of those variables was instituted as the workhorse of social policy (Oakes, 2003).

In the 1960s, the initial measures of racial differences between whites and blacks found stark differences and deep inequalities. At the slow pace at which progress was being made, it would take several centuries before blacks would achieve equity with whites (Fein, 1966). Critics were quick to point out that comparing races without regard to class differences was like comparing apples and oranges. So a new form of research began "controlling for social class." Controlling means that investigators carefully compared only African Americans, whites, and other groups who had the same socioeconomic backgrounds, namely, income, education, or both. A third measure, occupational prestige, was derived from the general regard the public had for specific occupations, how well each occupation paid, and the general difficulty of entry into each occupation. Combinations of occupational prestige, income, and years of education have been used ever since as standard measures of socioeconomic status (SES) (Nam, 1965).

The best way to show racial progress was for a new and expanded black middle class to develop. So it was no coincidence that middle-class blacks were discovered by the mid-1970s. Now, for face-saving reasons, there was a class of African Americans to compare with the majority white middle class. Furthermore, the specific contribution of race to inequality could be isolated by "controlling" for social class differences. Racial differences could finally be measured precisely and independently of class. But more important, a rapidly expanding black middle class suggested progress in eliminating racial inequality.

What Is Missing in SES

The full range of prewar qualitative factors that constituted socioeconomic differences by race is missing in postwar quantitative research. The following is a brief review of several of these factors.

Family Economic Circumstances

Take two people with the same income, the same level of education, and the same occupational status (class is controlled). One is from a family that is economically well-off, and the other is not. Without extraordinary motivation and luck, the person from the less-well-off family is likely to have fewer long-term opportunities and will be poorer financially by retirement. In the first place, starting out with unequal resources and with less to invest in education means it is unlikely that these people will start their careers with the same incomes, education, and occupational prestige. But if they do, the diverging abilities of their extended families to support these young adults will probably show up decades later in different economic outcomes (Blau and Graham, 1990).

For example, the capacity of one family to provide a down payment for a child's starter home alone confers a long-term advantage over the individual from a family that is not able to do so. The ability of one family to assist in paying for a graduate degree confers a long-term advantage over the person who has to rely on loans and who will sustain greater debt for his or her education. The means of one family to pay for its grandchildren's tuition and to enrich their formative years confers a long-term advantage over the family that is unable to pay for grandchildren's tuition and enrichment (Orr, 2003). These young adults may start at the same income, education, and occupational prestige, but because of their family's differential economic backgrounds, they are unlikely to have the same long-term outcomes.

Family Job Contacts and Knowledge

Take two people with the same income, the same level of education, and the same occupational status—again, class is controlled. One is from a family that is well established in a professional field or has members who are very knowledgeable about the profession; the other is not. The likelihood of receiving mentoring and sponsorship, making the right moves, making fewer mistakes, and "fast-tracking" is more likely for the person with family contacts and knowledge than for the one without. Over time, the person without the family advantage is less likely to be as well off as the person with the advantages (Chiteji and Stafford, 1999).

The Ability to Exercise Influence over Political Authorities

Again, take two people with the same income, the same level of education, and the same occupational status. One is politically well connected; the other is not. Or one is from a family that is politically well connected, and the other is not. It is doubtful that twenty to thirty years later the person who started out with the political connections will still have the same income and occupational prestige as the person without the connections. The one with the connections will be better off.

Financial Resources Other than Income (Wealth)

Wealth is not income or the money one lives off of day-to-day. Wealth is the accumulation of assets (a combination of equity in one's home, savings, stocks, bonds, whole life insurance, income property, undeveloped land, and gems) that can be converted to money if necessary. With sufficient income-bearing wealth, one can live off the interest; the principle remains unspent and is left to increase in value over time. Take the same two people with the same income, the same level of education, and the same occupational status. One has personal wealth; the other does not. It is easy to guess who will be better off financially in time. And equally important is the fact that children from families with wealth have more opportunities for upward mobility than children from families without it (Avery and Rendall, 2002; Chiteji and Stafford, 1999).

Spouse and Spouse's Family Wealth

Even an individual who has no personal wealth or lacks access to contacts and knowledge among family members still may gain a financial edge from his or her spouse. A person's prospects of improving long-term SES can change by virtue of marriage and the financial status of a spouse's family. Wealthy in-laws can put a down payment on a house, finance advanced education, serve as an alternative to debt, and pay for a grandchild's tuition. They may also have professional contacts and special knowledge that one might not have access to if one had not married into the family.

Unearned Advantages and Disadvantages

All of these situations have one thing in common: they identify socioeconomic advantages and disadvantages that are not individually earned. The three conventional measures of SES (income, education, and occupational prestige) focus only on individual achievement. The additional components of socioeconomic status are derived from family economic and human resources upon which the individual can draw to gain relative advantage over peers who do not have the same family advantages. This is precisely where contemporary differences exist between the black and white middle class and other classes as well.

The conferring of social status also is intergenerational; it is inherited in the form of wealth and access to power, or the lack of both. A person does not achieve social standing in a single generation simply through his or her own accomplishments. From the findings of long-term holistic studies of communities and the social class differences within them, it is difficult to ignore family and generational differences inherent in socioeconomic status. Ironically, since the 1970s, most of these factors have been measured in a variety of surveys. But they are still not integrated with income, education, and occupational prestige to formulate more comprehensive measures of social class.

Without the missing prewar factors in SES, social scientists have not assessed social class and its impacts on US society thoroughly. In addition, measures of racial progress are incomplete. What were the full SES circumstances of African Americans and white Americans in 1965? We really do not know what impacts the War on Poverty or affirmative action have had on racial inequality and class differences in and between races. To what extent have black-white differences within the middle class been reduced since 1965? We do not know what the real differences are between Black America and White America. The impact of contrasting racial treatment over time exists in precisely the aspects of SES that have not been developed and could not be measured just by income, levels of education, and occupational prestige.

Social Class Values

There is an additional and very important SES factor remaining—social class values. It is assumed in the social sciences that each social class and its internal divisions are distinct sets of social values—defined as the meanings people give to their relative economic advantages or disadvantages (Centers, 1961; Kohn, 1969). Despite the strong desire among social scientists to test the prewar insights on social class, by 1960 no consensus had been developed on how one might measure social values—one of the more difficult qualitative social class dimensions to measure. Prewar qualitative studies pointed out that these social classes are coherent clusters of people largely because of variations in their values, not simply because of their education and income. This work has been advanced today primarily in political and marketing research (Michman, Mazze, and Greco, 2003; Robinson, Shaver, and Wrightsman, 1999).

The concept of social values was derived from Warner's method of isolating social classes (Warner, Meeker, and Eells, 1960). There were two certainties. First, there was a small group of people who were obviously rich, powerful, and well off who stood at the top of the social order. Second, there were the poor, least powerful, and worst off economically at the bottom of the social order. With regard to values, the goal of Warner's research team was to discover any breaks or clusters on the continuum between the obvious top and bottom of stratification. The "value" breaks that Warner found in Yankee City and that Drake and Cayton found among blacks are described below. These are the value dimensions of social class left out of postwar quantitative measures of social class that have not been tested for.

Upper-Class Values

Of utmost importance to the US upper class (those at the top of Warner's hierarchy) is the continuity of their economic privilege and high status across generations and not simply within their generation (Baltzell, 1958). They have their wealth and plan to keep this wealth for their children, their children's children, and so on. In order to accomplish their goal, the upper class must find ways to retain their major influence, if not outright control, of the central institutions that impact their group advantage—the economy and the government (Baltzell, 1962; Domhoff, 1974). Therefore, an essential class value is to manage financial institutions and major corporations and to hold high political office. The members of this class must exercise power in order to preserve and then advance family assets that are the basis of their wealth across generations. Each generation must at least preserve the wealth (assets) of the prior generation and ideally increase it. It is an unspoken rule that one must never live off of or spend down family assets, because these assets are worth millions of dollars to future generations and are the basis of future family privilege and status.

One way to see these values in operation is upon the death of an upper-class family patriarch in comparison to the death of a middle- or working-class patriarch. In the upper class, the value is that the estate and family assets are never divided among the children as they are among working- and middle-class families. Instead, family members in each generation who best reflect the class values and who can best manage the family inheritance take control of the (extended) family assets or designate an outside expert to do so. Noncontrolling family members, especially those individuals who do not yet reflect the appropriate values, only get allowances. The amount of a specific allowance is at the discretion of the family manager, paid only if there is enough money generated in interest from the family's principle assets.

Placing this kind of value on asset preservation is not an individual or single family activity. If it were, it would be impossible to exercise power and maintain privilege over generations as a group. Rather, influence and control of institutions and a focus on asset enhancement are group activities. Therefore, it is necessary to maintain close social ties and communication among upper-class families and to control class membership. Upper-class social boundaries are maintained not simply as an act of exclusivity or snobbery; they are essential to maintaining class political and economic advantages. So members socialize together, go to school together, intermarry, hire one another's children, and provide each other with essential business and investment information. Ideally, intermarriage within the class is an important way to enhance intergenerational wealth. An elaborate network of country, golf, yacht, and private clubs and social registries exists to maintain the upper class. Wherever they go in the United States or the world, members know "who is" and "who is not" in the class. Those who wish to marry outside the class or who reject the class values are cut off from trust income and inheritance.

Warner pointed out that the longer one's family has achieved the intergenerational feat of asset preservation, the higher one's status is within the upper class (Warner and Lunt, 1941). There are even intra-class divisions within the upper class: an upper-lower, an upper-middle, and an upper-upper. The upper class has done such a good job of masking its transition from a visible aristocracy to a business elite that some scholars now deny its existence altogether (Aldrich, 1988; Christopher, 1989). Others point out that this group still very much exists, with a few additions and losses (Pessen, 1973; Pessen, 1974; Zweigenhaft and Domhoff, 1998).

The pre–World War II US upper class was not a group into which a person automatically gained membership based upon his or her achievements within a single generation. That only happens in the middle class. One's family had to show appropriate ability not only to create wealth (above and beyond income) but also to preserve it over at least two generations. It is said that "anyone can make a great deal of money in their lifetime," but what distinguishes "quality people" from those who are not is their ability to preserve wealth and advance it across generations. To spend down and eventually lose one's wealth, and therefore forfeit the next generation's inheritance, is inconsistent with upper-class values.

The general public may consider people with lots of single-generation money, such as movie and rock stars, professional athletes, and rags-to-riches corporate executives, as the rich upper class. But to "old money," those people are only amusing and rarely show the right stuff—intergenerational longevity.

The central concerns and values of the pre–World War II upper class are foreign to the majority of white Americans, and there are *no* identifiable African Americans in this social class. The black "upper class" that Drake and Cayton described was upper class only by virtue of being at the top of the black social hierarchy. If these same people were in the white social hierarchy, they would have been only middle class. The top class of blacks was "upper class" in name only. Studies of black elites historically show that their values were close to those of the white upper class and that there was some intergenerational maintenance of middle-class standing (Cromwell, 1994; Moore, 1999). Even if those black elites had been permitted to cross the racial class line, however, their wealth would not have been stable enough and large enough to qualify them as part of the white upper class with which they shared nearly the same values. Ultimately, the black elite had to rely upon professional and educational resources for their class standing, which made them only middle class. By the way, this old black aristocracy is not what E. Franklin Frazier referred to as a "black bourgeoisie" (1957); the bourgeoisie were the newest, first-generation members of the black middle class who were there only by virtue of education and who did not possess the old aristocratic values (Landry, 1978; Teele, 2002).

Middle-Class Values

To Warner, this was the class of achievement. One entered the prewar middle class through education and professional/occupational achievement. Fundamental middle-class values included delay of gratification, control of consumerism, and a willingness to work hard and long toward a promised goal. These practices were valued as necessary ways to achieve sufficient education and occupational position to merit higher status and privilege and to enjoy life at a higher level, once established. Saving money, avoiding debt, and maintaining good credit were also valued as ways to advance and stay ahead materially. The discussion in Chapter 1 showed that historically this class has been heavily dependent upon a stable and predictable economy. Its members do not want to sacrifice and work hard to improve their economic position and then see the economy they are dependent upon disappear. Likewise, the middle class places a high value on social and financial contracts; one's income, and ultimately one's social position, is heavily dependent upon others fulfilling their promises.

Unlike the upper class, the prewar middle class valued an open social system—for white Americans. Class boundaries were drawn around those who demonstrated achievement and merit. One was recognized as "middle class" by demonstrating "respectable behavior." So it was important to know how to eat properly in public, how to dress like ladies and gentlemen, how to speak to peers and elders, and how to behave with members of the opposite sex. There were rituals that marked middle-class respectability, such as men removing their hats when entering public buildings or when eating, holding doors open for ladies, and not appearing improperly dressed in public. It was generally recognized that the more Americans who could become middle class, the better. It should be noted that this value dimension of the middle class predated the US middle class and has been studied extensively in early English society (Hunt, 1996).

Money alone did not make one middle class. It was possible to have very little money and still be middle class as long as one behaved appropriately, lived within one's means, and had little debt. "Respectability" without money was also clearly recognized among blacks. Working-class and lower-class blacks could be respectable as well; this is one of the paradoxes of black life (Dent, 2000). The top and bottom of economic stratification among blacks were close to one another. Being characterized as middle class was so new for each generation in the black middle class that a commitment to middle-class respectability and the demonstration of appropriate behavior were sufficient to mark middle-class boundaries. The primacy of respectability without money was as much the case for whites as it was for blacks and was the subject of equally unflattering descriptions, as in E. Franklin Frazier's *Black Bourgeoisie* (1957), Sinclair Lewis's 1922 *Babbit*, and William Whyte's 1956 *Organization Man*.

Working-Class Values

The prewar working class was described as the class of physical work. In economic stratification, these people were the craftspersons, supervisors, foremen, and top laborers among builders, movers, operatives, and instrumentalists. They were firefighters, police officers, and hands-on civil service employees. They valued direct hands-on involvement and "real" work rather than work from some desk and distant office. Following directions and doing what one was told was valued over questioning authority or independent thinking. This class orientation had a strong enough pull and its members were strongly enough committed to it that they sometimes would reject opportunities to become upwardly mobile into the middle class—what Blau and Duncan referred to as "cross-generational occupational solidarity" (1967:54).

Those who were still undergoing assimilation from European ethnic backgrounds were generally associated with working-class value orientation and a sense of working-class social class loyalty (Gordon, 1963). So it was never clear from the prewar community studies to what extent the working-class value orientation was based upon social class or ethnicity (Warner and Srole, 1945). Members of the working class were distinguished by consistent employment and relatively high-paid jobs compared to the larger lower class. A number of writers referred to union members in the working class as "the aristocracy of labor."

Lower-Class Values

Almost as soon as William Lloyd Warner's term *lower class* became popularized as a description of those at the bottom of society, people began to find ways to avoid being so described. No one wanted to be called "lower class," and for good reason. Very few prewar students of community spent much time studying those at the bottom. Much of what passed for the values of the lower class were middle-class stereotypes about its members' laziness, immorality, sexual looseness, ignorance, and lack of refined behavior. Because so many African Americans were in the lower class, Drake and Cayton focused more attention on this class among blacks than did other students of prewar US community. Drake and Cayton never lost sight of the economic and racial restrictions that were at the heart of the behaviors they described. The structural impact of lower-class circumstances was very evident: the less work there was and the lower the pay, the more "disorganized" were the behaviors of the workers and those in their immediate community (1945).

What Drake and Cayton described as the lower class and Warner described as the lower-lower class were people who had temporary and the lowest-paying work and who were severely restricted in housing choices (due to ethnicity, race, and class). Few knew of others in their community who were paid less or were worse off. Those at the very bottom were more likely to have insufficient food and to live in overcrowded housing. They lacked privacy and experienced continuous stress at home and at work that often led to violence. Stealing to make ends meet or out of a sense of injustice meant that many people in this class spent time in jail. Heavy drinking was used as a form of mental escape. Men did not make enough income to support families and be a financial head of the household, so marriage came late, and separation and divorce were common. In addition, if they were black, they were "the last hired and the first fired." More often, men earned less than women who were doing domestic, laundry, and service work, a situation that in turn led to domestic conflict and role reversal—independent women and dependent men. This in turn led to men's exaggerating their sexuality in order to maintain their sense of masculinity and their need to have control over women. Their response to poverty also led to temporary and casual sexual relationships and common-law marriages and resulted in women having babies without ever marrying the fathers.

Ironically, the values of the lower class are the most difficult to isolate and describe. Those who live at the bottom of society long enough will develop their own culture and coping mechanisms designed to survive poverty and the external constraints imposed on their lives (Valentine, 1968). For example, they may value having children whether they are married or not and whether they can financially support them or not. They may value extended family life with parents and siblings over their nuclear family life with their husband or wife as their primary source of mutual support. They may value entertainment, dance, music, humor, and expressiveness in clothes and behavior as necessary ways to relieve stress and forget their worries.

What some described as lower-class behaviors and values were compelled by poverty and economic marginality. Warner was well aware that class-based coping behaviors among whites came from their ethnic backgrounds (Warner and Srole, 1945). Likewise, African Americans drew upon their southern rural background and what was left of African traditions.

At this point, the key question to ask is what a more comprehensive analysis would look like and what it would it show us. The following section presents an illustration.

Implication of Missing Values in SES

Each social class is described here as if the classes have distinct and mutually exclusive core values. This is only for the purpose of description and explanation. None of the prewar students of community argued such a point. It was understood that social classes were points on a continuum. The upper class had the strongest boundaries and was the most difficult to enter. In contrast, the middle, working, and lower classes merged into one continuum. There were individuals who were complex mixtures of different social class circumstances and values; there were people in one social class whose values reflected another. Some people appeared to inhabit two classes at once and held multiple sets of class values simultaneously with all the inherent contradictions. Furthermore, during a person's lifetime it was possible to start in one class and end up in another.

The prior discussion may seem a long way from the black middle class and its context within US social class, but it is very central to understanding the new black middle class. The role of values is a classic issue in understanding any social class and goes back in the social sciences to Emile Durkheim, Karl Marx, and Max Weber. A classic question is: to what extent do social values make economic mobility possible, or how can social values retard progress? Durkheim demonstrated that the Protestant north of eighteenth-century Germany was more prosperous and economically more dynamic than the Catholic south. He asserted that this was because of the greater value that Protestants placed on individual initiative and risk taking. Max Weber codified these values as the "Protestant work ethic" and hypothesized that the Protestant ethic was the basis of the dynamic economic growth in northern European and, by extension, all capitalism. In contrast, Karl Marx proposed a class consciousness compelled by the proletariat's material circumstances. This consciousness was in direct conflict with the ruling class and would counter capitalism and its resulting inequities.

A lot more is involved here than a classic intellectual argument. There are practical issues at stake that are central to the middle-class experience and to social science research. The bottom line is: to what extent do people have control over their class circumstances by virtue of their values? Out of this question comes a number of hypotheses. Some assume that if someone is in the lower class, but acquires working- or middle-class values (Protestant ethics), then it is more likely that this person will move up in social class. A lower-class person who has middle-class values will be upwardly mobile over a same-class peer who maintains lower-class values. This assumption regarding values and class is a truism within the US middle class and a virtual religious belief in the black middle class. The counterhypothesis is that social mobility is structured. That is, the economy defines one's opportunities or lack of them, regardless of one's values. This means that after one's material circumstances change, one's values change—not the other way around. For African Americans, the additional concern is the removal of racial restrictions to allow equal participation in the economy.

Missing Factors Behind SES

The limits of the current formulation of SES become very apparent when one looks systematically at factors that can influence variations in social class. What SES reflects in current research is the cumulative influence of several factors that post–World War II research has lost sight of.

What follows is an illustration of the impact of several prewar factors on education, one of the three main SES variables. Some 4,344 respondents in the National Opinion Research Center's General Social Survey (GSS) between 1998 and 2002 were asked background questions related to social class mobility and values. There were three social value measures—religion (the extent to which one believed in a religious faith), affinity to Marxism as a social value (the extent to which one agreed with some key Marxist propositions), and affinity to Weberian values or the Protestant ethic (the extent to which one agreed with several individual fate and responsibility questions). Then there were such measures as race (white and black), father's socioeconomic index (PASEI), mother's socioeconomic index (MASEI), and spouse's socioeconomic index (SPSEI). The socioeconomic indices were composite scores based upon a 1989 GSS study of occupational prestige (Nakao and Treas, 1992).

Figure 5.1 is a path analysis of the impact of these background variables on education. The numbers in the boxes represent standard scores—measures of the extent to which variance in one variable is accounted for by variations in the other variables. Note that the relationships between religion and values and between race and socioeconomic indexes (SEIs) are reciprocal (covariates); the arrows between variables are double headed. The relationships among education, values, and SEIs are causal; the arrows are one-directional.

The relationships between the two sets of value statements and education were weaker than the relations between education and the socioeconomic indices. This means that parent's and spouse's SEIs have a greater impact on a respondent's years of education than do the respondent's social values. Those who report higher levels of religiosity are more likely to favor Weberian values (Protestant ethic) than Marxist (opportunity is limited and structured). The relationship between father's SEI and race is much stronger than the relationship of race with mother's and spouse's SEIs. The relationships between race and SEIs are all negative—the higher the SEI, the more likely it is that the respondent is white. Overall, only about 15 percent of the variance in education is explained by values and SEIs. This means there are potentially more powerful and yet to be identified variables that might

Figure 5.1 Relationships Among Factors Influencing SES, Black and White Respondents

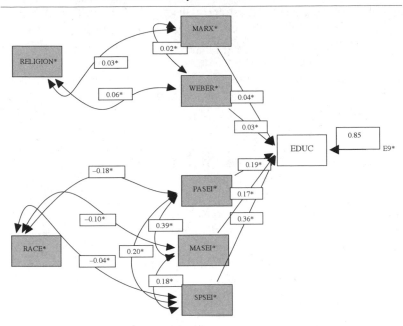

Note: EQS model, Chi Square = 15.42; P = 0.35; CFI = 1.00; Root Mean Square Error of Approximation = 0.01; E = the residual associated with the measurement of each observed variable.

account for the remaining variations in a respondent's education. From this analysis, we get a sense of the extent to which education as a component in SES can in fact be an intermediate variable in a complex relationship with other variables not directly accounted for in SES.

A repeat of the same analysis (see Appendix) with only white respondents shows only one difference from the analysis above. Religiosity is equally associated with favoring Protestant ethic attitudes (Weber) and Marxist attitudes. As in the overall analysis, parent's and spouse's SEIs better account for variance in education than do values. Black respondents in a third analysis (see Appendix) showed different relationships in comparison to whites. The higher their religiosity, the less likely they were to favor the Marxist propositions and the more likely they were to favor the Protestant ethic propositions, but the relationship of the Protestant ethic was weaker than it was with the Marxist belief. It is interesting that the strongest relationship between Weberian values and education in all three analyses was with black respondents. In the third analysis, only the relationship between the spouse's SEI and education was stronger.

These path analyses illustrate that variations in SES, which have been so important to explaining differences in countless postwar studies, are influenced by unaccounted-for background factors. SES is a proxy or covariate in a complex web of self and family background factors. In this complex web, a family's material resources and social relationships account for a respondent's variations in SES more fully than just a respondent's social values.

Implications of Incomplete SES for Obscured Social Classes

The path analyses above suggest a need for a more critical look, not only at black social classes but also at the conceptualization and measurement of social class in US life. There are subtle but important differences in the background variations in white and black SESs. Making the black and white middle classes equivalent based just on education, income, and occupational prestige ignores real differences between these two classes.

Uncritical use of these three factors alone has led to viewing the black and white middle classes as indistinguishable. Yet increasingly, contemporary literature about the black middle class portrays it as anything but indistinguishable from whites. African Americans who have been to the right schools and are in well-paying and prestigious occupations still report experiencing racial discrimination, being the object of racial stereotypes, and having to fight uphill against presumptions of inferior preparation, motivation, and qualifications (Collins, 1997). They describe having to carry an unfair personal burden and responsibility that their white peers could not imagine—referred to as a "black tax." Yet none of this is picked up or is evident in either the measurement or interpretation of SES.

In social policy and social research, the inner world of the black middle class is reduced to income, education, and occupational prestige and is made equivalent to the white middle class. But it turns out that limits in how social science looks at blacks extend to its analysis of the larger mainstream middle class as well. In effect, limitations in the consideration of the black middle class are also limitations in the investigation of social class in US life. Based on an equally critical look at the social class literature since the 1960s, we do not know any more about the inner world of the white middle-class experience than we do about that of the blacks.

Implications of Contemporary Studies

The movement to redefine the qualitative prewar community studies of social class arose out of questions about the validity of the descriptions. The totality of classic prewar literature on social class constitutes a world of hypotheses for quantitative reexamination. The Cold War and McCarthy eras in the 1950s undoubtedly diminished enthusiasm for the study of social class differences. In addition, the civil rights movement and the subsequent need to show a reduction in racial inequality delayed once again the promise of revisiting Warner's and Drake and Cayton's class descriptions. This research still needs to be done to advance and better understand social class in contemporary US life.

Chapter 4 reviewed the distinct black social class that Jim Crow built. This chapter has explored the background of the black middle class from Jim Crow to the contemporary era. In this transition, the black and white middle classes became comparable by socioeconomic measures, despite their historical and intergenerational differences. The next chapter will explore the basis for the new black middle class, challenges to its existence, and its vulnerabilities. Again, we will find all three of these issues in question in the mainstream middle class as well.

6

From Affirmative Action to Diversity

The contemporary black middle class did not come into being out of business and enterprise; rather, the growing number of blacks in white-collar jobs and the expansion of the black middle class after 1960 are products of government regulation and intervention as they were in 1866.

Origins of a New Black Middle Class

The 1964 Civil Rights Acts and presidential Executive Order 11246 constituted the foundation of a new black middle class, just as the Civil Rights Act of 1866 had set the stage for the first. Jim Crow and formal racial segregation had to be dismantled in order for an expanded black middle class to come into existence. The Civil Rights Acts may have started the process by ending formal Jim Crow and other legal forms of racial discrimination in US. Even more critical in the rise of the new black middle class, however, was Executive Order 11246, which required affirmative action in the hiring of African Americans. It put into motion the actual mechanics by which education, government, and the private sector would be desegregated, nationally and not just in the South.

There are very few African Americans today in the professions, management, or any other white-collar work who have not directly benefited from affirmative action in college admissions and in hiring after college. In this sense, the contemporary black middle class can be called the "affirmative action" middle class. There are black professionals who would object to this point. They are now too distant from affirmative action's formative period. These individuals would lead one to think that one morning in the late 1960s, a generation of poor, hard-working, deserving, and highly qualified African Americans suddenly emerged out of nowhere. Through their individual hard work, virtue, and high intelligence they succeeded in spite of their communities. Martin Luther King Jr., Malcolm X, the civil rights movement, urban riots, or affirmative action had nothing to do with who they are and where they are professionally. No doubt many of these critics have all the personal qualities required to succeed and are hard workers, but what they do not appreciate is that their talent would not have been recognized and their hard work would have not been rewarded if the opportunities had not been there for them in the first place. What they do not understand is that their talents and hard work did not create their initial opportunities; the doors were opened by people and movements that came before them.

Authorizing affirmative action was not the only cause for an accelerated growth of the black middle class. If that had been the case, Executive Order 11246 would have been one of the most remarkable pieces of statecraft ever. The reversal of 100 years of formal and informal black racial exclusion from the mainstream of US life could not have happened simply because the president of the United States ordered it. This change occurred because a temporary national consensus emerged supporting racial desegregation as an outcome of the civil rights movement and of Martin Luther King Jr.'s persuasiveness. This consensus was driven primarily by the national press and by national religious, labor, and educational leaders based upon public policy precedents set as far back as the Great Depression. That was when the nation had dealt with a crisis similar to civil rights, that of the emerging labor movement in the 1930s (Boris, 1998; Graham, 1990; Moreno, 1997).

The 1960s national consensus in support of affirmative action was far more important than Executive Order 11246 and had a much greater impact. Universities and colleges began to make conscious efforts to recruit and admit black students *before* government "affirmative action" regulations were fully formulated and implemented. Businesses and government agencies also were more deliberate in their efforts to recruit and hire black employees *before* formal affirmative action measures were adopted. These efforts were initially self-motivated and only by the end of the decade became referred to as "affirmative action." It took almost ten years for this wide range of outreach, admissions, and hiring practices to be formalized and integrated into general admission policies and student services in higher education and into what is now called human resource administration in business and government. It was in this period from 1964 to 1974 that there was a hastening of blacks into the nation's middle-class mainstream (Blackwell, 1987; Freeman, 1976).

Between 1970 and 1977, blacks in white-collar jobs increased from 10 percent of black labor to 13 percent (US Census Bureau, 1979:74, 248). In seven years, there was as much progress as in the prior decade. Black college student enrollment more than doubled nationally; blacks made rapid progress toward parity with whites in the professions. Racial disparities declined between black and white Americans in income, education, and a host of other factors. It was at this point that it became clear that there was an emerging black middle class with very different roots than the older black middle class that had evolved under Jim Crow. It was also at this point that William Wilson (1978) suggested that race was of declining significance based on evidence such as that in Table 6.1.

If changes in white-collar work among black workers are good indicators of changes in the black middle class, then improvements continued after 1977. The 1990 and 2000 census measures of managerial and professional work are not quite the same measures as those used prior to 1990. But even as approximations, the proportion of blacks who did white-collar work continued to increase after 1977. In fact, the Reagan decade saw more rapid progress in blacks' attaining white-collar jobs than had the prior decade, even with conservatives' attacks against affirmative action. Table 6.1 suggests that progress during the 1980s matched

Table 6.1   Number (in thousands) and Percentage of Black and White Employed Workers 16 Years and Over Who Did White-Collar Work and Their Ratio, 1970–2000

	Employed Blacks	% Black White Collar	Employed Whites	% White White Collar	B/W % Ratio
1969	947	11.3	17,796	25.6	.44
1978	1,907	17.4	23,658	27.5	.63
1988	1,781	15.3	27,409	26.5	.50
2000	3,576	25.9	36,578	35.3	.73

Sources: 1970 to 1978 data are from US Census Bureau, *The Social and Economic Status of the Black Population in the United States, 1790–1978,* vol. series P-23, no. 80 (Washington, D.C.: US Government Printing Office, 1979), pp. 74, 248; 1988 data are from US Census Bureau, *Statistical Abstract of the United States: 1990* (110th ed.) (Washington, D.C.: US Government Printing Office, 1990); 2000 data are from US Census Bureau, *2001 Supplemental Survey Summary Tables,* PCT049B, PCT049A (http://factfinder.census.gov).

progress during the Clinton era, the 1990s, a period of rapid national economic growth. The disparity between whites and blacks doing white-collar work was narrowed from a ratio of less than one black worker for every two white workers in 1970 (.43) to three black workers for every four white workers in 2000 (.73). This suggests very solid progress toward racial equality in middle-class employment.

If one looks no further than white-collar work, it would appear that "victory" in the racial dilemma is at hand. The mainstream press, influenced by conservatives, has already made such a declaration. A liberal interpretation might suggest that in another one or two decades at most, racial parity in white-collar work will be achieved and federal affirmative action could be dismantled. For affirmative action to go on any longer would transform acting affirmatively into entitlement that has run its course (Davies, 1996). But given the precarious history of the black middle class, this is hardly a complete picture. The first black middle class, more than 100 years ago, was destroyed after similar gains. Like the bedrock of any class, the black middle class is based upon a continuation of the conditions and the circumstances that called it into existence in the first place. If these circumstances disappear, then new props must be found, or the class will crumble as it did before. A closer look at the underlying mechanics for continuing the black middle class is in order.

A Troubled Context for Progress

It is premature to celebrate the new black middle class. Instead, it poses a paradox because its rapid rise is virtually the only good news on the black-white racial front in the United States since the 1970s. By 1990 non-middle-class blacks were more racially segregated than they had been at the height of Jim Crow segregation in the South or during the 1960s urban riots (Massey and Denton, 1993). There has been virtually a complete failure to end racial inequalities (disparities) in health, primary and secondary education, crime, teen pregnancy, housing, and unemployment. With a black middle class, the belief can be trumpeted that US society is a land of opportunity regardless of race. Without a black middle class, it would be evident that black-white relations in the United States are racing backward to a new and de facto Jim Crow era. Without a black middle class it would be hard to hide the fact that this nation has not solved its historical racial dilemma and is not a land of opportunity for all Americans.

Opposition

Gains in black attainment have come with intense opposition from predictable sources. It is no coincidence that the same congressmen who opposed the Civil Rights Act in 1964 were the spiritual leaders of opposition to affirmative action and were still major influences in Congress in the new century. The two most visible were former Democrats who turned Republicans: Strom Thurmond and Jesse Helms (Cohodas, 1993; Griffin, Evenson, and Thompson, 2005). The goals of states' rights, the need for smaller (weaker) federal government and lower taxes, and the preference for individual initiative and conservative morals were all articulated by southern congressmen before they became the national agenda of neoconservatives.

A second deep pool of opposition to affirmative action is found in the white lower middle class. White ethnics in Chicago provided a preview to their opposition to black advancement in their racially graphic demonstration against Martin Luther King's only civil rights march in the North. When affirmative action was implemented, they became the shock troops of conservative opposition with charges of "reverse discrimination" (Cowie, 2002; Durr, 2003; Formisano, 2004; Freeman, 2000). Furthermore, the white lower middle class has had a long history of opposition to union efforts to bring about racial equality (Nelson, 2001). The members of this class, as the sons and daughters of immigrants, do not feel that inequalities in US history should be corrected at their expense; doing so essentially negates their sense of the American dream (Clark, 2003). Prior to World War II, they compromised the growth of the union movement by opposing blacks, Latinos, and immigrants as members. Their opposition to black advancement goes well beyond perceived threats to their jobs; the bottom line is that their sense of racial privilege is threatened so much that one writer suggested that they have an "entitlement disorder" (Hall, 2004).

Since the 1960s, as during Black Reconstruction, opposition to affirmative action has intensified and grown increasingly effective. The admissions of the first cohort of black students and the hiring of the first group of black employees in the 1960s triggered debate over procedures and qualifications. How many blacks were going to be admitted or hired? What were their qualifications? How would they "make it" in the university, college, or business worlds if they were any less qualified than their white peers? What were whites to do who were not admitted or not hired if "less qualified" blacks were taking "their" places? Questions concerning the qualifications of the white critics were rarely asked.

At first, questions about black qualifications coexisted with flexibility in admissions and hiring. Unexpectedly, opposition to affirmative action provided universities and colleges, businesses, and public agencies with an opportunity to recognize how they really operated. Before 1960, people were admitted, rejected, hired, and promoted for reasons that often had little to do with their qualifications, training, competency, or merit. Prior to affirmative action and especially before World War II, all-white universities and colleges were more like social clubs than formal institutions. People were admitted or hired because of who they were, who they knew, and whether they had money and family connections (Synnott, 1979; Wechsler, 1977). Prior to desegregation in 1964, admissions and hiring procedures were much less formal and transparent. Anyone recommended by the right person and able to pay the tuition could get into the majority of universities and colleges in the United States. Even admissions to elite institutions were not nearly as competitive as they are today. Businesses and government agencies routinely recruited at favorite schools and hired the friends and relatives of current employees and managers.

By 1975, opposition to affirmative action had become more insistent; then the opposition went to court. The 1976 United States Supreme Court case of *Regents of the University of California v. Bakke* challenged the practice of using racial set-asides. This was a strategy, ironically encouraged by Republican president Richard Nixon (Kotlowski, 1998), in which a number of institutions practiced affirmative action by setting aside a percentage of admissions slots for black applicants. The result was a dual admissions system in which whites competed for regular admissions and blacks competed for the set-asides. In the *Bakke* case, the United States Supreme Court outlawed set-asides but permitted race to continue as a factor in admission and employment decisions.

The End of Affirmative Action

The charge of reverse discrimination by whites and the Supreme Court's scrutiny of affirmative action did more to end the national consensus in support of acting affirmatively and voluntarily to end racial discrimination than the Court's *Bakke* decision. Affirmative action continued after 1980, but primarily because of federal mandate rather than as part of a favorable consensus among national leaders. It is my contention that affirmative action for African Americans grew markedly less effective after the *Bakke* case. While attention was on *Bakke,* another development helped reduce the effectiveness of affirmative action for blacks.

The civil rights movement also sparked "liberation" expectations among Native Americans, Mexican and Puerto Rican Americans, Japanese and Chinese Americans, the disabled, and white women. Soon, all of these groups claimed they too had histories of discrimination and were underrepresented in higher education and in the professions—the main criteria used for rationalizing affirmative action. So they were brought under the umbrella of affirmative action, and blacks became one of many "targets of opportunity." By 1980, affirmative action was used to correct the underrepresentation of women and racial "minorities," not just to deal with black inequality.

The point is, the very tool initially used to correct black inequality in the 1960s began losing its effectiveness for stimulating black progress during the 1980s in the Reagan years. As a result, other less obvious factors became very important to sustaining black advances in higher education and in the private sector. By 1990, a critical mass of black alumni and students had evolved in most historically white colleges and universities, and these groups have maintained pressure on their universities and colleges to continue recruiting black students. Blacks in government service and in companies and corporations have provided information and created networks for other blacks seeking work and have pressed their departments and businesses to recruit African Americans. At the same time that affirmative action was being crippled from outside of higher education and business, this inside impetus to sustain it was overlooked and underappreciated. Members of the new black middle class themselves became a factor in sustaining their progress.

Beginning of Diversity

There is another factor in sustaining black progress after 1990 as affirmative action's effectiveness waned. Besides the presidency of Bill Clinton, which was favorable to affirmative action, an alternative motive has emerged for continuing the black middle class. Businesses have developed greater sophistication about both consumer markets and national demographics (Lynch, 2005). Continued growth in business is increasingly dependent upon expanding markets. African Americans and other nonwhites are an increasing proportion of the nation's population and of businesses' potential consumer base. To effectively market to an increasingly diverse consumer base, one's workforce has to be equally diverse. At least a symbolic black presence has become important to businesses' financial bottom line. Likewise, college and university trustees and administrations at elite institutions have come to realize that if future leaders are going to reflect the nation's racial and cultural diversity, they must train their share of these leaders. People of color have become increasingly important in student enrollment–driven state college and university admissions. Government services have realized the same thing. A diverse workforce is a source of unique and varied talents and perspectives needed for organizations to be effective. It is increasingly necessary to have a diverse middle-level workforce to stay in business in a demographically diverse society. Diversity has replaced affirmative action as a rationale and motivation for maintaining a black presence in the nation's institutional life.

Maintaining some black presence in business and education has happened despite conservative efforts to end affirmative action. Conservatives believed that the passage of the 1996 California Proposition 209 would end affirmative action in California. Proposition 209 amended the state constitution to prohibit public institutions from discriminating based upon race, sex, and ethnicity and is commonly interpreted as banning affirmative action. They hoped 209 would spark a national revolt at the state level. Studies of white popular support for Proposition 209 explored whether this support was due to "old-fashioned" racism, was based on a perceived economic threat, or was more symbolic in nature (Alvarez and García-Bedolla, 2004; Sawires and Peacock, 2000; Tolbert, 2003). All three were found to explain white support for Proposition 209. Opponents of Proposition 209 predicted dire consequences, but to conservatives' dismay, their "victory" has turned out so far to be an empty one.

Despite the example of Proposition 209 in California, efforts throughout the nation to maintain the presence of blacks and other minorities continue with little disruption, and an effective movement in other states to ban affirmative action has not materialized. The transition to diversity as the underlying motive and rationale for acting affirmatively is also evident in two 2003 Supreme Court cases, one involving admissions at the University of Michigan Law School, *Gnitter v. Bollinger,* and the other admissions in the University of Michigan College of Arts and Science, *Gratz v. Regents.* To the surprise of many, the nation's other elite universities, several of the nation's largest corporations, and even the US military joined with the University of Michigan to support the use of race in admissions decisions. They argued that using racial identification was necessary in their efforts to achieve a diverse student body and workforce. Diversity was necessary in order to effectively educate, provide services, do business, and equally distribute the burden of defending the nation.

The transition from affirmative action to diversity has been confusing to both supporters and opponents of affirmative action. It turns out that Proposition 209 had more to do with stigmatizing any form of government action to address racial inequality than correcting any actual or perceived abuse. Most Californians who favored Proposition 209 do not realize that federal affirmative action regulations continue, even in the Bush administration, nor do they understand that affirmative action ceased to be effective for blacks years ago.

After Proposition 209 passed, black applications and admissions to the highly competitive University of California (CU) system declined. But they also briefly declined at the California State University (CSU) system even though the CSU system is much less selective, and minority students do not need affirmative action for admissions (National Public Radio, 2006). An example of the confused state of affairs is that at one state university campus a faculty selection committee refused to consider a highly qualified African American candidate for a faculty position to teach African American history because affirmative action had been "outlawed." After opposition by black faculty to this crude application of Proposition 209, the university administration cancelled the search, and it was repeated with closer supervision by the new "diversity officer."

But there is something very different about diversity when compared to affirmative action, again evident in the University of Michigan Supreme Court case. The diversity motive is not about maintaining or creating an effective tool to correct racial inequality from the past or in the present. The central argument for maintaining race as a factor in admissions and hiring is that it is in the best interest of universities and businesses. Affirmative action was designed initially to correct inequalities for black people, but it is now about the interests of universities and businesses. Ironically, diversity protects the rights and opportunities of universities, corporations, and the military. Diversity is not about redressing generations of racial discrimination and continued underrepresentation of blacks in US life.

The Diversity Black Middle Class

The diversity black middle class, which is unlike the Jim Crow middle class and actually may be like no other, certainly fulfills Max Weber's definition of a social class. Its members are conscious of one another and of their status above working- and lower-class blacks. They socialize with one another around this common awareness. Like the preceding group, they have something Max Weber did not conceive of: besides social class consciousness, many have racial consciousness as well. They are very much aware that they are not part of the white middle class and that race is their primary social reality. Their social status and social milieu have been created apart from the black masses and are dependent upon the fairness and willingness of whites in power to play by the rules for promotion, job evaluations, awarding of grants, tenure and retention, seniority, and due process. If whites simply looked out for themselves, the new black middle class would quickly disappear.

Karl Marx's dismissal of the petite bourgeoisie also applies to the diversity black middle class. They do not own or control the "means of production," nor are they a proletariat or a vanguard of the working class. In the Marxist worldview, they serve at the pleasure of the "ruling class" to administer, supervise, train, guard, counsel, and produce goods and services to maintain the social system and those in power. The diversity black middle class is literally a shadow of the US white middle class. At the same time, the diversity black middle class is solidly part of the historic bourgeoisie, and its fate is dependent on the success or failure of the current social and economic system.

The diversity black middle class quickly exhausts insights derived from Weber and Marx. Of classical theorists, Richard Tawney came closest to describing the new black middle class (Howe, 1992). It was clear to him that class in the modern world combined both economic reality, as in Marx, and social status, as in Weber. So classes are based on their economic condition or "relation to the means of production," and they are also hierarchies of varying social statuses conditioned by history, lifestyle, and other noneconomic factors. Again, for the United States, these other powerful factors are ethnicity, religion, and race, which are a lot more complex and subtle in their influence than a great many social scientists acknowledge (Hamilton and Form, 2003). Tawney recognized exactly what the black middle class does. It plays a professional and systematic role in the larger society and economy, and then members of this class go home to "wear the costume appropriate to (its) hours of ease" (Howe, 1992: 10). Here "costume" is ethnicity or racial culture, and "hours of ease" are one's social world apart from one's public, work, and professional worlds. The black middle class, like other classes, has the ability to have multiple identities and to live in conflicting worlds simultaneously.

The basis of the diversity black middle class's standing is first and foremost service to the larger society. This is most evident for blacks who supervise (hire, train, evaluate, and fire) whites and provide professional services to whites. In the civil rights integration ethos, they have fully "arrived" and represent the race well by showing that blacks can qualify for and do the same jobs that whites do. This symbolic participation and role modeling is foremost. Colin Powell and Condoleezza Rice in the George W. Bush administration are excellent examples of this symbolism and modeling. The mainstream press never asks of the few blacks in influential national roles: "Whose interests do you advance or retard by your professionalism and devotion to duty?" In contrast, this point is debated in the black press because it is not clear that most blacks benefit from their presence and work.

Black middle-class service to the larger society is also apparent when one looks at teachers, social workers, doctors, and others in the helping professions who provide direct services to other blacks. All of these professionals work in the public sector of federal, state, or local government or in the private sector for nongovernment national and community-based agencies. Middle-class blacks now serve black people as professional employees of the state and of state-regulated agencies. They do not set policy to determine who they can or cannot serve and how; legislators do that. Nor do they determine funding. White professionals familiar with the social class and racial culture of their black clients can do the same jobs.

The diversity middle class's role of providing services has similarities to that of the Jim Crow middle class. Prior to desegregation, the majority of blacks were literally the "bread and butter" of the old black middle class. If the black majority's social and material circumstances improved or deteriorated, so did the circumstances of the Jim Crow middle class. If the lower and working classes were out of work, the middle class would suffer as well. The middle class received increased income through increased black consumer and retail spending and other blacks' increasing ability to pay for personal services. It is not clear that this linked fate still exists between the black middle, working, and lower classes today. The relationships among the three black classes is now mediated and defined by federal, state, and local government employment.

The social class circumstances of the diversity middle class necessitates collective action on only one basis—to strengthen and advance its members' own class position and status in the larger society. Middle-class blacks will come together to talk about their work, to form professional associations, to network around careers, and to find new job openings. For those who have not forgotten their roots, affirmative action is a virtual religion—for what should now be obvious reasons. But coming together around the social and economic plight of non-middle-class blacks is not reinforced by their social class position. When and if members of the black middle class address racial inequality, it is out of race consciousness, not because of their social class.

Furthermore, the diversity middle class has very tenuous ties to its predecessor. In fact, many hold contempt for the Jim Crow black middle class. The affirmative action and diversity middle classes are just completing their first generation. Most of its members are from the working and lower class and have memories of their and their parents' experiences with social exclusion, color prejudice, ridicule, and even opposition to their advancement from members of the older (Jim Crow) middle class. It was particularly traumatic for those who had their character and life potential judged by black "gatekeepers" based upon having darker skin color (Glenn, 1963; Hill, 2000; Seeman, 1946). Color is still very much a factor in black social stratification (Gullickson, 2005). The problem with this contempt is that it is now self-defeating because it now influences the way some members of the new middle class see the middle class and their role in it. In fact, many do not see themselves as middle class at all and are very ambivalent about their class identity when dealing with other blacks.

Finally, the diversity middle class is not a self-defined and self-regulated, cohesive social aggregate. It is more like a social amalgam around specific professional and job-related interests. Members do not define or control the criteria for acceptance and identification as either black or middle class. One can reject membership and involvement in this class with no adverse consequences. It is not necessary to be in a particular social sorority or fraternity, nor is it necessary to be a member of a particular church to be in the black middle class. Of course, there are members of the middle class who still insist on having traditional values, church affiliation, and social sponsorship into the appropriate clubs and organizations. But this is a far cry from the "upper" class that Du Bois, Daniels, and Drake and Cayton described. Those with traditional orientations in the first half of the twentieth century controlled who was admitted to the middle class, who was identified with it, and what constituted membership in the middle class despite its flexible criteria for membership. But today blacks with this traditional worldview are only one of several orientations in the contemporary black middle class.

Amid the transition to the diversity rationale from affirmative action, the black middle class will continue at least until conservatives formulate an effective attack against diversity. Much more can be said about the diversity black middle class, summarizing the extensive com- mentary of others about it (Dennis, 1995; Dent, 2000; Fulwood, 1996). But an assessment of this class's place within general social stratification is what is needed most. As mentioned in Chapter 1, discussions that focus solely on the black middle class outside of the context of mainstream social stratification are of limited utility and in fact obscure the real dynamics and changing realities of black life in the United States.

In the first part of this chapter, the proportion of blacks in white-collar employment was used as an indicator of growth of the new black middle class. This single measure can provide only a one-dimensional and therefore incomplete picture of the black middle class. Additional comparative measures provide a superior multidimensional view; a more complete picture follows.

Educational Attainment

The single most important ticket into the modern middle class is higher education. Given the lack of family inheritance and wealth, education is even more important for blacks than for whites. When white colleges and universities opened their doors to blacks after 1965, black student enrollment more than doubled, and their graduates could go on to white-collar professional, technical, and managerial work. The expansion of black college enrollments was extraordinary. But what does this achievement look like when it is compared to white student enrollment? Based upon conservatives' charges of reverse discrimination, one would think that growing numbers of white students were denied college admission because less-qualified black students were "taking their places."

The fact is the majority of colleges and universities in the United States have virtually open enrollments. Of the almost 3,000 institutions listed in any of the popular and comprehensive guides to colleges and universities in the United States, less than 6 percent are identified as "selective" or "very selective" in their admissions. In other words, if you apply and can pay the tuition, you are admitted to most colleges and universities. Less than 5 percent of all US institutions of higher education are selective, and only 1 percent are very selective. Furthermore, the assumption that all private colleges and universities are of higher quality than state colleges and universities is false. There are "nonprestigious" state universities that have more competitive admissions and offer an education superior to that of many "prestigious" private colleges and universities. What these private schools have over their state peers are more carefully crafted public images. They are "prestigious" so that anxious middle-class parents can buy educational status for their children, most of whom are only average academically and do not have the grades and test scores to get into the nation's selective colleges and universities. So they go to discreetly nonselective "prestigious" institutions with others like themselves who are not particularly interested in learning and who need a little time to mature before going on. Figure 6.1 gives the reader a sense of the extent of the celebrated increase in black enrollment relative to white enrollment since 1955.

The surprise in Figure 6.1 is not that there have been so many more white college students than blacks, Hispanics, and Asian-Pacific students. The surprise is that this figure shows that between 1955 and 2002, white college and university enrollment grew at a much higher rate than it did for blacks. Black enrollment began its upward movement in 1967, appeared to peak in 1977, went up very slowly in the 1980s, increased in 1993, and then increased slowly again until 2001. In comparison, white enrollment increases have been robust since 1955 and sharply increased in 1995. This tells us that increases in black enrollment attributed to affirmative action happened when the number of institutions and the gen-

Figure 6.1   College Enrollment by Race, 1955–2002

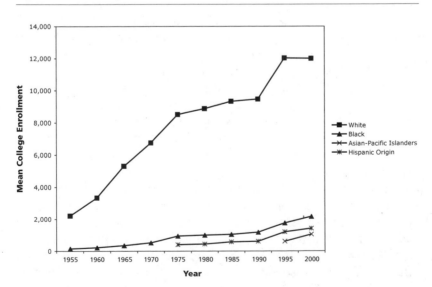

Source: US Census Bureau, 2004a.
Note: Mean numbers are in thousands.

eral capacity of higher education were expanding rapidly. Whites over-all have given up nothing to blacks and other minorities. In fact, one could argue that many colleges and universities have turned to blacks and other minorities to help fill their classrooms and to maintain enroll-ment. This is especially the case at state institutions that receive enroll-ment-driven funding. They must recruit from a population base that in-creasingly consists of blacks and other minorities. Demographics and the need to fill institutional capacity have trumped affirmative action, at least since the 1980s.

Enrollments tell one story. What do bachelor's and advanced degree completion rates add to this picture? Figure 6.2 provides another dimen-sion to the comparative context of black attainment in higher education.

The percentage of blacks who have completed four or more years of college has steadily increased since 1974. The percentage of whites who have completed four or more years of college also has grown steadily in the same period. Both lines reflect rising attainment; the upward track

Figure 6.2 Percentage, by Race, to Complete Four or More Years of College, 1974–2001

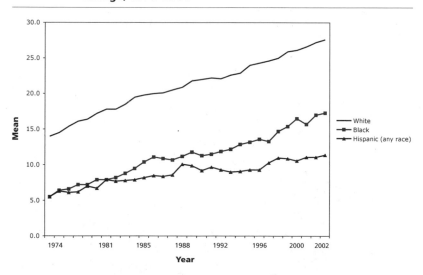

Source: US Census Bureau, 2003.
Note: The mean difference in college enrollment rates between 1975 and 2003 is 8.55 per-centage points, df = 44, p < .001.

for blacks is virtually identical to that for whites but on a lower scale. The news here is that between 1974 and 2003, the rate of increase in degree attainment for blacks is not higher than it is for whites. The image of blacks gaining in education achievement is correct, but these gains have not reduced the gap between black and white degree attainments. Hispanic college attainment has been falling in comparison with blacks and whites.

Disparities in Income

If higher education translates into middle-class occupations, how do the incomes of black degree earners compare to those of their white peers? Figure 6.3 provides this picture (Census Bureau, 2004b). Over the twenty-eight-year period between 1975 and 2002, whites with four or more years of college education earned on average $30,434; blacks with the same educational attainment earned on average $24,385. Paralleling educational results, black income levels between 1975 and 2002 have risen along with white incomes and have virtually the same track. There

Figure 6.3   Mean Earnings of Bachelor's Degree Holders by Race and Year

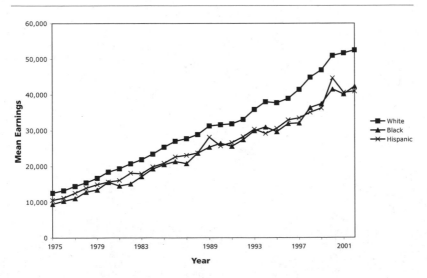

Source: US Census Bureau, 2004b.
Note: The mean difference in income between 1975 and 2002 is $6,049, df = 27, p < .001.

appears to be a slight divergence in black and white incomes over time, but there is no statistical difference between them.

Blacks with four or more years of college education and presumed middle-class employment have a persistent gap between their earnings and that of their white peers.

Perhaps we are not looking closely enough at educational attainment. Advanced degree holders are people who have maximized educational achievement as a ticket into the middle class. The presumption would be that the earnings of black advanced degree holders are comparable to their white peers, but Figure 6.4 shows that they are not.

A different pattern is evident from this comparison than those shown in Figures 6.2 and 6.3. White advanced degree holders earned on average $43,083 between 1975 and 2002, whereas their black colleagues earned on average $33,482 in the same period. Incomes for black and white advanced degree holders tracked upwardly together until approximately 1997. Then the black income line dropped almost $5,000, whereas earn-

Figure 6.4   Mean Earnings of Advanced Degree Holders by Race and Year

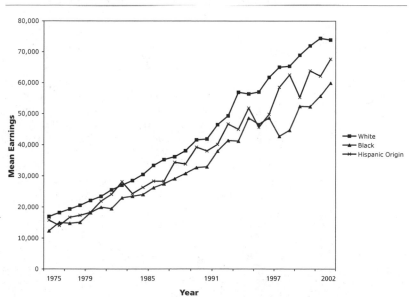

Source: US Census Bureau, 2004b.
Note: The average difference for twenty-seven years is $9,601; the rates are statistically different at p < .001, df = 27.

ings for whites continued upward. The next three years (1998–2000) saw some recovery in income for blacks, but black earnings are now following the white rate with greater divergence than was the case prior to 1998. Perhaps this can be accounted for by the well-publicized end of affirmative action in that same year as well as retrenchment in US corporations, a situation that negatively affected blacks holding white-collar jobs more than it did whites (McBrier and Wilson, 2004).

Disparities in Wealth

Maybe the celebrated advancement of the black middle class is evident in the top fourth quartile of family incomes. If you divide family income into quartiles and compare black earnings with white earnings between 1970 and 2000, there has been no real progress in closing the racial income gap in any quartile, nor was there any black progress in the top 5 percent of incomes (see Table 6.2). The black-white family earner ratios hardly changed at all. It is as if the progress of the 1960s and the affirmative action gains of the 1970s had never happened.

Table 6.2   Black and White Average Income by Quartile, 1972–2000

	Number of Families (thousands)	Upper Level (in $) of Each Fifth				Lower Limit, Top 5%
		Lowest	Second	Middle	Fourth	
Blacks						
2000	13,174	$11,726	$22,991	$37,294	$59,000	$105,373
1990	10,671	6,456	13,732	24,000	39,100	69,265
1980	8,847	4,190	8,170	13,500	22,084	37,000
1972	6,809	2,456	4,612	7,375	11,800	18,800
Whites						
2000	80,527	$19,800	$36,000	$56,156	$86,648	$153,230
1990	75,035	14,275	25,710	38,676	58,022	99,156
1980	68,106	8,383	15,161	22,744	32,750	52,316
1972	58,004	4,486	8,360	12,098	17,150	27,472
Ratio Black to White						
2000	0.164	0.592	0.639	0.664	0.681	0.688
1990	0.142	0.452	0.534	0.621	0.674	0.699
1980	0.130	0.500	0.539	0.594	0.674	0.707
1972	0.117	0.547	0.552	0.610	0.688	0.684

Source: US Census Bureau, 2006a.

As was described in Chapter 5, wealth is not considered when defining middle-class membership, but variations in wealth between the middle and upper classes are real markers of class differences. Intergenerational wealth and the ability to maintain it distinguish the upper from the middle class. In order for the black middle class to be comparable in any way to the white middle class, its members must be peers in wealth as well as in income. Table 6.3 is a comparison of married two-earner black and white families by income and wealth. It is based upon analyses by Oliver and Shapiro (1995:97) of the 1984 Survey of Income and Program Participation (SIPP) data.

In 1984, on average for every three dollars married blacks earned, their white peers earned four dollars (ratio .77). For young couples and all two-income couples, the difference in black-white incomes was narrower; the black couples earned four dollars for every five dollars the white couples earned. Oliver and Shapiro highlighted younger couples (twenty-five to thirty-five years old) in their analysis to see if their income

Table 6.3   Race, "Middle Class," Families, Work, and Wealth, 1984

	Income	Net Worth	Net Financial Assets
Married			
White	$32,400	$65,024	$11,500
Black	$24,848	$17,437	0
Ratio	0.77	0.27	—
Two-earner couple			
White	$40,865	$56,046	$8,612
Black	$34,700	$17,375	0
Ratio	0.85	0.31	—
Two-earner young couple[a]			
White	$36,435	$23,165	$1,150
Black	$29,377	$4,124	0
Ratio	0.81	0.18	
White collar[b]			
White	$34,821	$48,310	$8,680
Black	$34,320	$7,697	0
Ratio	0.70	0.16	—

Source: M. Oliver and T. Shapiro, *Black Wealth/White Wealth: A New Perspective on Racial Inequality* (New York: Routledge, 1995), p. 97.
Notes: a. Twenty-five to thirty-five year olds; b. does not include self-employed.

ratio was lower than the overall. If so, this would have been an indication
of potential for future income parity. There was no difference. But when
they looked at black-white racial income among professionals, technical
experts, and managers in the SIPP data, near parity was apparent in income. This evidence matches the results shown in Tables 6.1 and 6.3
based upon census occupational statistics. This is the good news.

The bad news is that comparisons of wealth of blacks and whites
show what might be the greatest disparity of any US federal statistics on
race. Overall, in 1984 white Americans had an average net worth of
$46,000, whereas black Americans had an average net worth of $4,400
(ratio of .095). For every dollar that blacks had in net worth, Whites had
ten dollars (Oliver and Shapiro, 1995; "Whites Own Ten Times the Assets of Blacks," 1986). In the majority of cases for both whites and
blacks, their wealth was in the value of their homes and in retirement
funds (Keister, 2000). Table 6.3 shows that the wealth ratios for the
black middle class are better than the overall rate, but there is still a vast
difference in wealth between races. Black married couples have a worth
of approximately one-quarter that of whites; net worth is three-tenths
for two-earner black couples, one-sixth for young two-earner black couples, and the same for white-collar black workers. The last point is significant. In the SIPP data, blacks in white-collar jobs have nearly eliminated the income gap between them and their white peers, but they
have nowhere near the same in wealth.

The last column in Table 6.3 shows the average net financial assets
that black and white earners have available, given their net worth. If
these families were suddenly without jobs, this is what they would have
to live off of until they rejoined the labor force. Table 6.3 shows that, on
average, blacks in the middle class have nothing to fall back on. With
regard to wealth, the racial differences between black and white Americans overall, and in the middle classes in particular, are vast and without comparison.

Impact of the Growing Underclass

There are other factors that put the new black middle class into perspective. Another reason the ratio of black white-collar workers to all blacks
in the workforce improved after 1980 is that they are compared with a
smaller and smaller proportion of other blacks in the workforce. The
workforce is like an elevator; the fewer passengers on the elevator, the
more obvious one's presence. US government statistics include in the
workforce only those who have jobs or are actively looking for one. If

one is not actively looking or has not found a job in fifteen weeks, one is not counted as part of the labor force; these people disappear from federal labor statistics.

An unspecified number of blacks in the working and lower class have had such difficulty finding work that they are no longer counted in the labor force. Other blacks have stopped looking altogether, with the same outcome. The net result is that blacks in white-collar management, professional, and related fields are not being compared with all blacks who potentially would be in the labor force if it were not for the fact that they are discouraged workers. Blacks in white-collar jobs are compared only with those officially in the labor force. If blacks who have dropped out were counted as well, the ratio of blacks in white-collar jobs to all blacks in the workforce would be lower. The more blacks who drop out of the labor force, the larger becomes the proportion of blacks in white-collar employment when compared to all black workers.

Explanation

Along with attacks against affirmative action, there is an increasingly in-fluential cottage industry of private public policy and research institutes and consultants whose role is to explain away in the press racial dispari-ties in educational attainment, family income, wealth, and labor force par-ticipation (Rich and Weaver, 2000). They have taken up where Daniel Patrick Moynihan left off in his infamous 1965 report on black families in the United States, *The Negro Family, the Case for National Action.* Conservative interests through black spokespersons argue that these dis-parities exist because of deficiencies in black family life, community, leadership, and morals (Elliott and McCrone, 1987). They claim that racial discrimination, racial prejudice, and institutional racism no longer exist. So, whites no longer can be held accountable for whatever racial in-equality still exists in the United States (Asumah and Perkins, 2000).

The new Moynihans also argue that a number of nonracial factors now explain the persistent gap in white-black incomes. Blacks are more likely to select social service and teaching careers than whites; these jobs pay less. There are proportionately more black women who have attained four or more years of education than black men; women's salaries are generally lower than men's. Many black students and, in particular, black males do not value education, are opposed to it, and are unwilling to work as hard as whites and model Asians. Proportionately more black than white professionals live in the South; salaries are generally lower in the South than in the rest of the United States. Conservatives' explanations for racial disparities have been most convincing when they come from other blacks. According to the new critics, middle-class blacks who support affirmative action have yet to show that they have what it takes to really be middle class (Asumah and Perkins, 2000; Sowell, 1975). These same critics rarely question the qualifications of whites in the middle class.

What has been shown above is that there still exist real racial disparities among middle-class blacks and whites. So even those who have demonstrated self-discipline, who have received an education, who have the values necessary to work in the professions and in management, and who are potential role models for other blacks have not achieved economic equality with their white peers. Furthermore, based upon trend lines going back as far as 1940, there is no evidence that the future will see equity even for the black and white middle classes without some unforeseen drastic differences in national policies and practices.

Implications for Blacks

The increasing number of blacks in white-collar jobs as an indicator of the growth of the black middle class is the basis of the celebration of racial progress since 1965 and the declaration of the declining significance of race. This measure of progress is one dimensional in two ways. First, it is one dimensional because the rapid growth of the black middle class is based upon its proportion among all blacks. Second, it is based on change in only intragenerational individual achievement. A multidimensional picture would also compare family material and human capital within and across the prior generation as well as wealth. A multivariate view would show a more complete picture.

Another key contextual factor not fully appreciated in prior analyses is the rapid growth of the middle sector in western societies since 1940 (Zunz, Schoppa, and Hiwatari, 2002). There has been a tremendous expansion in white-collar work and a related rapid expansion in the college-educated workforce, as shown in Figure 6.1. This expansion was going on for more than two decades before racial desegregation in the 1960s. In effect, black "progress" was made in the wake of an unprecedented expansion of the middle class. Allowing black participation in such an economy via affirmative action did not require real sacrifice of positions or of privilege by whites. One could even argue that some racial progress might have happened even without affirmative action. The need was so great for white-collar workers that some blacks would have been recruited anyway to partly fulfill the need.

There have been strong indications since the early 1990s that the need for the US middle class is waning and that the economic price of remaining in the middle is rising (Phillips, 1993). What will happen to the black middle class when the rapid growth of the US middle class ends, as we may be witnessing today? If there is a 10 percent decline in the middle class over the next decade, will there be just a 10 percent decline in the black middle class? Clearly the black middle class shares the same fate as the white middle class. But the continuing reality of racial discrimination against blacks and of privilege for whites likely means that there will be no equal distribution of pain when times get tight. The number of blacks in the middle class will decline faster and earlier than the number of whites. Blacks' current marginal status in education, income, and wealth virtually guarantees earlier black declassing. The more the white middle class struggles, the more African American participation in the middle class will be called into question. It does not matter whether continued black participation is rationalized through affirmative action or diversity. The charge of reverse discrimination and unfairness to whites will take on a harder and harder edge, aimed precisely at the black middle class.

Those who are familiar with the history of black participation in the US economy are not surprised with a prediction of increasing opposition to a black presence in the middle class when economic growth stalls and reverses. There have been repeated examples in history when blacks were "the last hired and the first fired" (Cantor, 1970). It is false to assume that somehow the new black middle class is exempt from this history. Most recently, the post–World War II gains of the black working class occurred at the end of almost a century of industrial growth. As soon as blacks became well employed and established in urban industries, companies started laying them off, moving, retrenching, automating, and closing facilities owing to obsolescence. Blacks were the last hired and first fired. Likewise, we have experienced almost half a century of college-educated middle-sector growth. This growth was well underway when blacks were permitted to enter the mainstream middle class after 1965. But now, the party is over. There may be no more rapid growth for the domestic US middle class; continued rapid growth will be overseas in emerging economies. Wherever retrenchment occurs, the black middle class will be reduced first. Blacks will be the first pushed out, if for no other reason than the fact that they have on average zero net financial assets—last hired and first fired.

The data in the tables in this chapter show that the black middle class is not the equal of the white middle class and illustrate how a one-to-one individual comparison is inappropriate. Individual blacks may compare well with individual whites with regard to income, education, and employment. But when blacks in the middle class, however it is defined, are grouped and compared with whites by wealth, the advantages and disadvantages by race are apparent. This is precisely why the rise of the new black middle class is an inappropriate measure of racial progress in the United States. The class has made progress only against other blacks, not against its white peers. Therefore, the need to address racial economic inequality in the United States remains. No one should be surprised. The civil rights movement led to the elimination of legal and formal racial segregation; it was prevented from challenging racial economic inequality.

How can blacks receive the same education, income, and employment as whites and on average still lag economically? The US tradition is to blame the individual. Critics of affirmative action and diversity (any basis for black presence) rationalize that blacks apparently are not, in fact, as well educated or as responsible with their income or do not work as hard as whites. In which case, any direct effort to support a black presence in the middle class does a disservice to whites because blacks do not deserve it. But a whole class of people does not wake up one morning deficient in talent and skill anymore than they wake up with a full-blown Protestant work ethic. Americans fail to appreciate the extent to which unresolved racial and social class inequalities and remaining advantages and disadvantages from the past are carried over into the present. Affirmative action for blacks was not in place long enough and was not allowed to evolve into an effective and precise enough tool to wipe out the long history of racial advantages for whites and disadvantages for blacks.

Implications for Whites

Many readers will wonder who is in the white middle class I am referring to in this book. White readers see themselves as struggling to make ends meet as well. They do not see that they have more wealth and assets than blacks. In using the same analysis here for the white middle class, this bewilderment can be addressed. The size of the black middle class has been overestimated, but so also has the size and wealth of the white middle class. Oliver and Shapiro (1995) and other students of race and wealth do not separate the white middle class from the white upper class in their estimates of white wealth. If they were able to, I would estimate that the net worth of the average person in the white middle class might not be much higher than it is for blacks.

White upper-class wealth and middle-class wealth are combined in the studies on race and wealth because that is what federal statistics do. The upper class is not separately reflected in federal statistics. The technical narrative for the only data that can distinguish wealth from income points out the following: the highest and lowest net worth families and individuals were undercounted (US Census Bureau, 2003).

But are not middle-class whites more competitive than middle-class blacks? Do they not have higher grades and test scores and, therefore, merit the jobs that blacks are getting? This would be a good point if one were describing apples against apples rather than apples against oranges. What this chapter points out is that middle-class blacks would compare well with middle-class whites who have one-fifth the net wealth of other whites and no net assets. The true white peers of most middle-class blacks are whites who are the first in their family to go to college and have no others in their immediate or extended family in the middle class. Black extended families with several college-educated members are as rare as they are common among white families. Furthermore, high grades and test scores are not the primary or sole criteria for admissions in the majority of colleges or universities for any group, nor are they the sole criteria for being hired for jobs in the United States. If this were the case, most whites would not be admitted or hired either, because they are only average. Other criteria for selection into colleges and universities and for hiring decisions are athletic ability, children of alumni, children of wealthy and influential families, those with talent in the performing arts, ability to speak a foreign language, being from a foreign country or another region in the United States, and being a particularly skilled and extraordinary person. Most accept these other criteria for admissions among whites without question. But when it comes to efforts to address racial inequality, many whites suddenly become well qualified and competitive, and these other criteria are immediately overlooked.

There is another obvious point that can easily be overlooked. In reviewing the context for black middle-class growth, the circumstances for the growth of the white middle class are also described. There is increasing recognition that the rapid growth of the middle class since 1940 is a direct outcome of federal policies and the growth of the corporate sector and that the size of the middle class is heavily dependent upon both (Edsall, 1992; Glassman, 2000; Skocpol, 2000). Blacks needed the affirmative action consensus and federal policy to participate in the growth of the middle class. Before affirmative action, however, whites had access to federal subsidies such as federal mortgage loans, mortgage tax deductions, highway subsidies, the GI Bill, federal student loans, and other federal domestic spending that helped generate a post–World War II middle class. The post–World War II white middle class did not come out of what so many political commentators and conservatives claim—individual enterprise in business. Most whites, like most blacks, are employees and are not small-business owners and entrepreneurs as was the classic middle class of the 1800s.

The main point to be taken from this chapter is that the black and white middle classes are not precisely comparable and that the black middle class is "barely in the house." The black middle class, however, is the weathervane of trends facing the larger middle class. The next chapter will take a closer look at how the black middle class has changed since the classic descriptions of the 1940s and what implications these changes have for the mainstream middle class.

7

Anatomy of Today's Black Middle Class

There have been changes in black social classes since Drake and Cayton's definitive study of black social stratification in Chicago in the late 1930s. The rise of the new black middle class is certainly one of them. This development does not stand apart from other changes. For one thing, the rise of the new black middle class has not protected it from the same downward mobility other black classes face. Their vulnerability and decline increase the black middle class's vulnerability and in a way that cannot be imagined across the race line. What follows is a proposed updating of Drake and Cayton's model based on changes in the sixty years since *Black Metropolis* (1945).

Changes in Black Class Structure

The lower, working, and middle classes still exist much as Warner defined them, but there is still no black upper class comparable to the white upper class. As in the 1930s, members of each class are conscious of themselves apart from others in approximately the same three divisions. Then, as now, none of these classes is completely separate from one another; their boundaries are fluid, running in and out of one another. For most, class and status have overlapped where the lower and underclass have the least status and the middle class has the most; status is still tied largely to one's occupation or lack of one.

In addition, the church-related, secular, and "shady" vertical divisions still exist as Drake and Cayton defined them. These three intra-class divisions run through each black social class. Secularists see the world in primarily economic, material, and political terms and associate with one another. "Shadys" in each class still make their living through illegal means, now primarily through drug trafficking, and associate with one another. Then there are still those whose lives revolve around their church; they too prefer to associate with each other. In sixty years, what has changed is the distribution of these intraclass subdivisions.

Divisions Within Each Class

According to Drake and Cayton, when moving down the social class system, the secular subdivision decreased as a proportion of blacks in each social class and the church-related and shady subdivisions became larger and larger. During Drake's and Cayton's fieldwork in the 1930s, the majority of blacks in the lower class had jobs. They had low-paying jobs at the bottom of the job market, but they had jobs, nevertheless, when compared to black joblessness today. In Bronzeville, the lower one's social class, the more likely it was that one faced poverty and survived through illegal work, although others dealt with the same poverty through the church. It was very difficult to be secular in one's worldview at the bottom of the hierarchy or to survive without having to become socially affiliated with either the illegal economy or the church world.

I would propose that today the secular and illegal subdivisions of each social class are larger proportions of the black lower class than of the other classes and that the underclass is a larger proportion of all blacks than was true in the 1930s. A media-driven commercialization of all goods and services in US life is now so pervasive that the boundaries of secularism have been expanded within black life and culture. This has led to a greater secularization of all black social classes than in the 1930s. The toll has been taken in the church-related division. Each successive generation after World War II has had proportionately fewer members who organize their lives completely around church-related activities. The trend is toward more black alienation from the church, and even those who subscribe to the church orientation are less intensely religious than their grandparents. In fact, the rise of black fundamentalism is a reaction to secularization. This may seem antithetical to the apparent omnipresence of churches in black communities and to the rise of megachurches. The other changes follow.

Professionalism

Today, behavioral criteria as the basis for class membership still hold, but those viewed as middle class and secular are expected to have a steady and well-paying job; preferably they will have a college degree and be in an appropriate profession. The most successful drug dealers are still part of the middle class and still cover their illegal activities with legal front businesses; they too see their work as a profession.

For example, black psychologists, doctors, dentists, and so on have their closest social ties with other black professionals. Family ties, generally in the working class, are still important, but more often one's closest social ties are with same social class peers in other professions. Furthermore, few in the black middle class still "party" and socialize as frequently and as intensely as did class peers in prior generations. Professional networking is the more important motivation for socializing, and this entertainment is more likely to occur at home in small groups. In this sense, the rapid increase in the number of blacks with a college education and a professional job has decreased the importance of behavior-based criteria as prerequisites for middle-class membership and identity. It has also decreased the necessity to socialize with families and across class boundaries.

Isolation

Another change in the internal organization of the black middle class is not unique to blacks. In pre–World War II research, respondents reported close contact with their social class peers—close enough that one could interview them and follow their social relationships from person to person through an entire social class. People in each class knew others both inside and outside of their class as neighbors, fellow churchgoers, and club members and acquaintances. People in the lower class and underworld also relied on each other heavily for survival through mutual exchanges of food, household appliances, clothing, and housing. This practice has continued and was observed as recently as the early 1970s (Stack, 1974). There were many passing contacts with people in other social classes as well. Residents in different social classes lived close enough that one could observe class differences even when these differences were more behavioral than material.

Yankee City and Bronzeville, when compared to today's urbanized communities, were more like small towns. It seems that one could not be in the middle class without social engagement with others in the same class. A person had to be known and accepted by peers before self-identifying or being labeled middle class. You could not easily self-identify with a social class that you were not a member of, as you can today. Today, affiliations in a social class and in subdivisions of social classes are voluntary and by personal choice. So objectively, one can be middle class but subjectively self-identify as working class; one can be working class and self-identify as middle class; and so on. Or one can deny having any social class altogether. There is no "community" that can force an individual to assume a specific social class identity or keep him or her out of a class in the eyes of others in the community. Nor is there any class outside of the upper class that can draw effective boundaries around itself. The same trend is apparent in mainstream US life and culture (Putnam, 2000).

Isolation also makes individuals less dependent on family and neighbors for their survival or social identity. People know fewer of their neighbors in their immediate community than they did a generation ago (Putnam, 2000). But this does not mean they are without social contacts. The people one has emotional connections with are less likely to live next door or down the street. Increasingly, for the middle class, they live in other neighborhoods, cities, or even countries; one's sense of community is no longer bound and defined by one's immediate physical space (McLean and others, 2002; Simon, 1995).

Drake and Cayton's presentation of social classes as a horizontally divided pyramid was not simply for the researchers' convenience. The pyramid indicated real interconnections and close proximity between social classes. The same interconnection and closeness are not evident in the contemporary literature on the black social class experience. The size, complexity, and diversity of community life today constitute a completely different environment than in the classical pre–World War II communities upon which the original social class concept was based. The point is that the experience of social class today, with the possible exception of the old-money white upper class, is much more fragmented and members are more isolated from one another. Upper, middle, working, and lower classes have their own neighborhoods and their own complete social worlds, however fragmented. These worlds may be now more rigidly divided by race than they were in the 1930s (Anderson and Massey, 2001; Massey and Denton, 1993). This means that when individuals see and experience others, they are almost exclusively in their own race and social class.

Media-defined Social Identities

Durkheim and Weber inferred that social class was based partly on social values; Marx asserted that social class was based on one's relationship to the means of production. Warner provided evidence that both sets of criteria were feasible, but contemporary US society offers yet another determinant of social class. In the place of real social contact and interaction there is increasingly the media—television, the Internet, and video games (Korzenny and Ting-Toomey, 1992; Perse, 2001). A consequence is that race and social class identities are increasingly defined by mass media rather than by direct social experience. If this is so, the middle or working class no longer exists as a fixed place or station in a collective consensus or on an economic continuum. One's social class experience is shaped by how one identifies with the racial and social class content of common electronic media, which blur personal experience and historic identities. As a result, people increasingly see, compare, and define themselves and others based on media characters and images. Now, one can have an imaginary identity and find others to affirm it.

Take all of these trends into consideration, and the middle-class experience is much less of a coherent social and group experience and is more personal and individualistic. The boundaries are still there, but they are much less apparent. One is never certain where one is relative to others or who one is in the minds of others. There is little overlap between one's subjective class standing and one's relationship to the means of production or one's allegiance to particular class values. One could assert that the black middle class exists largely as the media defines it and may now have little capacity to respond and say for itself what it is and what its reality is. This is because of the isolation of its members from one another in tight-knit relationships, the lack of ability to influence and sanction one another around class boundaries, and the omnipresent media that substitute sports, news, and crime shows for one's own realities. One reality for blacks rarely addressed in the media is just how close the black middle class is to the black working and lower classes and how dependent it is on them.

Expansion of the Underclass

Another change is the greater prominence of the underclass. In the early 1990s, there were three times as many nonpoor blacks as there were poor blacks, and the underclass was only half of the poor (Billingsley, 1992), yet the underclass exercised far more influence then its numbers suggest. As pointed out in Chapter 6, the increasing size and influence of the underclass is having a serious and negative impact on the black middle class. Although still a minority among all African Americans, the underclass appears to have expanded as a proportion of all blacks since

Bronzeville in the 1930s and since World War II (Glasgow, 1980; Massey and Denton, 1993). Why? The answer is not that blacks want welfare over work, are lazy, have and come from broken homes, and reject education for fear of becoming "white." All of these problems exist, but they are not causes, as the media has reported (Moss, 1979)—rather, they are symptoms. The real causes are much bigger—like the 500-pound invisible gorilla sitting in the room with us. The gorilla is the accumulated consequence of every failure since 1965 to reduce joblessness among blacks—the War on Poverty, the war on hunger, job training, school reforms, community mental health, and public housing. Liberals charge that these efforts did not go far and long enough, and conservatives respond that they were ineffective and wasteful.

Whatever is one's view on efforts to reduce joblessness among blacks, the consequences for the black underemployed and unemployed have accumulated for more than sixty years. High unemployment in urban black communities has gone on unchanged for more than two generations. The black unemployed have not simply been discriminated against and kept in low-paying jobs as they were in the Great Depression of the 1930s. An undetermined proportion of all blacks have been without work so long that they are no longer a part of the US economy. Unemployment does not mean that one does without income and no longer needs to eat, pay rent, and so on. It means that one must find an alternative way to make money to survive and live. If you cannot make a living legally, the only choice is to do so illegally—as Du Bois described in the Philadelphia of 1898, as Daniels described in the Boston of 1914, and as Drake and Cayton showed in the Chicago of the 1930s. The same is true today but with a much larger number of people. The new black middle class is matched by a new and largely expanded underclass. Black unemployment is unique today compared to any other time in US history. This is the first era in which black labor is simply not needed, a situation that was predicted by Willhelm (1971) and Yette (1971). Increasing numbers of blacks are simply not needed for any productive purpose. The new black role is to keep larger and larger numbers of well-paid police, judges, doctors, nurses, social workers, researchers, and prison guards employed with work that is virtually guaranteed through retirement.

Since 1965, drug trafficking has become the primary alternative economy and response to long-term high unemployment, unlike anything that can be imagined in a white community. It has yet to be explained why, but after the race riots in the 1960s, massive quantities of heroin appeared initially in the communities where blacks had rioted.

Nationally, heroin distribution was far beyond the ability of 1960s black criminal organizations; they had neither the money nor the know-how to set up such a massive endeavor in which thousands are addicted and involved in sales and distribution. If World War II and the civil rights movement had raised black expectations, the scope of heroin trafficking crushed the same expectations and utterly crushed black community life. Furthermore, drug trafficking in the United States on a massive scale was confined for more than thirty years almost exclusively to black communities, whereas small-scale and recreational use characterized white communities. The lowest-income communities with the most drugs were the least profitable for dealers, whereas white higher-income communities with recreational use were potentially the most profitable. This leads one to ask: if drug trafficking was simply about making money, why was it confined to communities where people had the least money to buy drugs? Some have suggested that there are people in the federal government who know more than the answers to this question (Webb, 1998). Only recently has drug trafficking started to appear in its own right in suburban white communities.

Based on community studies of the homeless and of drug users (Bourgois,1995; Sterk, 1999), a very different picture emerges than was evident in Drake and Cayton's *Black Metropolis* (1945). Today, drug dealers in black communities are simply the lowest-level employees in vast international cartels. This is quite different than it was in the 1930s, when dealers were independent businessmen and women. The old gangsters in Bronzeville had to be community minded. They exercised restraint in who was permitted into their world. They were discreet in how visible their activities were. They were mindful of strong community sentiment against them. In contrast, contemporary drug dealers are unrestrained in their willingness to exploit. In Bronzeville, a relatively small number of women worked as prostitutes; today, in marketing crack cocaine, every young woman in the community is a potential "toss-up" (sex worker) who can trade sex for drugs or money and extend a dealer's market. The goal of drug dealers is now to get as many residents as possible to use and pay for drugs. Furthermore, dealers have great pride in their work and have a worldview—if they do not do it, someone else will. They see themselves as no different than legal businessmen.

Another change is that the contemporary underclass is now not just a class unto itself: it has gone on long enough to produce its own subculture. A related change is that the underclass views itself as more authentic than and as superior to the middle class. In place of deference, there is now utter contempt. In fact, upward mobility into the middle class is viewed as "selling out." Members of the black underclass reject working-class behavioral standards and values, as well. They see the church and secular subdivisions of these classes as "hypocritical." The contemporary underclass is not Warner's lower class or Drake and Cayton's "underworld." They are not a Marxist proletariat because they are not in the economy and subject to labor exploitation. Nor are they "peasants" sitting outside the capitalist system waiting to be recruited by employers to discipline the wage demands of the proletariat. They have been left out of the economy so long that they reject civil society and those who are still in it.

If the underclass were small, and its culture were ignored, its impact on the black middle and working classes would be minimal. But this is not the case. Its influence goes far beyond its size because its fashion, language, music, and attitudes are heavily exploited and marketed by white-run record, media, and fashion corporations. Gangster rap music and videos, the fashion exemplified by drooping pants without belts, and comic television personalities with sexually explicit materials are inspired by underclass street life and drug dealing. Mainstream advertisers, record companies, fashion designers, and retailers are earning billions annually promoting black underclass cultural products. This mainstream commercialization of the black underclass poses a powerful negative influence on black working- and middle-class youth. Instead of being stigmatized or viewed as deviant, the black underclass has become the new standard of what is "black," the thing to be, a vehicle for public recognition and the only black class celebrated by the mainstream media and white youth.

It is not necessary to be a rocket scientist to know that the way to make the black underclass history is lots of jobs that pay living wages and that these jobs must be available for at least a generation (Wilson, 1987). This would not only turn around the slide of so many blacks into the underclass but may also be increasingly necessary for whites as globalization takes its toll. This is one place where effective federal-scale intervention is needed.

A New Social Division

Hopelessness, intense alienation, lack of real national leadership, drug trafficking, the human immunodeficiency virus/acquired immunodeficiency syndrome (HIV/AIDS) pandemic, and self-destruction among black youth (all symptoms) have produced powerful pressures within black life to create alternative cultural expressions. We have seen it before among white youth. The 1960s white countercultures were associated with the discontent of white middle-class youth. These young people rejected the materialism, hypocrisy, and sameness of white middle-class and suburban life. Most were children of parents who were first-generation middle class. The result was a wave of counterculture lifestyles that embraced personal freedom expressed through drugs, sex, explicitness, and free thinking. Their purpose was to "tune-in" to a higher consciousness and "drop-out" of their parents' social and cultural worlds. This impulse to reject the cultural poverty of contemporary middle-class life has now reached the African American middle-class youth.

African Americans in general have had a limited number of choices to use in addressing their subordination in US life. They can always retreat into the church and its ritualism; rebel by becoming gangster rappers and drug dealers; separate from the racist United States by becoming black cultural nationalists; conform to the dominant political agenda by becoming conservatives; or innovate around cultural expressions—music, sports, fashion, and lifestyle (Moss, 1991). Black youth have chosen to be innovative by creating a new social identity and lifestyle that is now called the hip-hop nation (Chang, 2005). This innovation is more than a passing phenomenon and is now an additional vertical subdivision in black social stratification.

Hip-hop

In the 1970s, hip-hop started as a movement against gangs, violence, and the drug world among working-class youth in the Bronx. Hip-hop is now an established counterculture and lifestyle among young African Americans. It provides young people from the working and middle classes a "positive" alternative through which to express their alienation from and rejection of popular culture and their parents' world (Chang, 2005). Hip-hoppers are distinct from and often confused with gangster rappers who also claim to be hip-hop. Contrary to gangster rappers, hip-hoppers look down on conspicuous consumption as a ghetto and middle-class norm. They do not reject education as an important life goal. Like prior countercultures, hip-hop is defining itself as it goes along. For example, in the later 1990s, it made more sense to wear African dashikis along with military desert boots, have Jamaican dreadlocks, be about peace, and have music projects than to project any mainstream middle-class images.

Put all of the black social divisions identified by Drake and Cayton together with the new division, and today one has a bewildering cross-cutting of Warner's original social class notion. The revised and updated model of black social class is illustrated in Figure 7.1.

The hierarchy is divided horizontally by economic social classes as in the mainstream of US society. There are lower, working, and middle classes but no upper class. Then, the economic divisions are cut vertically by lifestyle, worldview, and legal-illegal participation in the economy—church, secular, and the modern equivalent of the "shadys"—drug dealers and their workers. The secular vertical division is further divided in the middle and working class by the relatively new hip-hop lifestyle and below that in the working class by a self-proclaimed "ghetto" lifestyle. The vertical divisions in the lower class have not changed since Drake and Cayton; they contain the church or sanctified lower class and the nonchurch lower class. Parallel to and below the lower class is the underclass, which is essentially out of the mainstream economy and alienated from civil society, mainstream and black middle- and working-class values and worldviews.

Figure 7.1   Revised Black Social Class Hierarchy, 2005

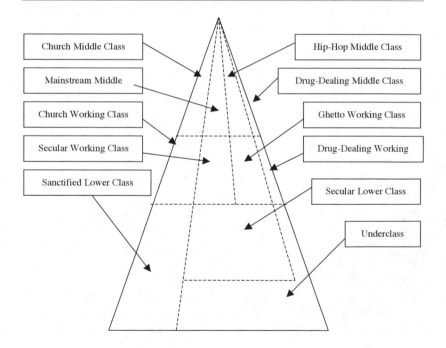

Impact of the Underclass on the Next Generation

Based upon raising young men and upon interviews of young adults, the apparent need of (black) youth to create for themselves an alternative social identity has a flip side—rejection of their parents' values. No place is the idea of black-white middle class comparability more questionable than in the rearing of young adults. Here the differences are inescapable; black middle- and working-class parents have a much greater struggle before them than their white middle- and working-class peers. White parents' struggle is to guide their children through a maze of popular images and help them to make the right choices. They have some positive popular cultural models to work with. In contrast, virtually all of the popular images that black youth have to choose from are from the underclass; their role models are pimps, drug dealers, sex queens, gangster rappers, sexually explicit comedians, stupid clowns, and assorted MTV rap video thugs. Furthermore, blacks who play these negative roles are not indifferent to the middle and working class; they are very clear in their contempt for both. For middle- and working-class black youth there are literally no other images that are "cool" and certainly none that affirm middle-class ideals and values.

In the underclass, pursuing academic goals and getting good grades also means being a "sell out." Black middle-class young people get this message, and if they behave like their parents, they are "sell outs" to their peers. Instead, white and black classmates alike expect them to be "down": to emulate the underclass and reject academic and middle-class social norms. Putting on "airs" is to show interest in anything outside of the experience of the black underclass and of what the corporations that promote the underclass culture celebrate as authentic "blackness." This is what black middle-class youth face, whether they go to predominantly black schools or to white suburban schools or live in black or white communities. Black parents must contend with a popular culture that is solidly lined up against their children's valuing and staying in the middle class.

In addition to a negative popular culture, black middle-class parents have a unique struggle with schools and teachers. Whether middle-class children are in public or private schools, many white and black teachers and administrators expect less of black students than they do of whites. What black children are universally expected to excel in is sports, whether the children have talent or not. There is hardly a black middle-class parent in the United States who does not have a tale of going to school and having a confrontation with teachers and administrators over their children's education or lack of it. This is a battle with long odds and lots of frustration; more often their children, who are conflicted about being middle class and simultaneously wanting to conform to lower social expectations, reinforce the teachers' low expectations against their parents' wishes.

No one wants to be in the shoes of black middle-class parents. West Indian first-generation immigrant parents seek to avoid African American culture for good reasons—their children's success (Waters, 1999). It is no coincidence that the children of British West Indian immigrants on average have higher incomes than African Americans (Kalmijn, 1996). Africans and West Indians are more likely to be higher achievers than their African American peers precisely because their parents are able to insulate their children from a racist popular culture that celebrates the most degenerate elements in black life. They do this by frequent visits back to the home country, and they remain in close contact with extended family that still has the old culture. This negates any cultural ambivalence about achievement that their children may have picked up in the United States. Now that the US South and even rural areas are fully integrated into US culture and media, African American parents no longer have a cultural "place" to send their children so they too might escape racism in popular culture and schools.

There are other challenges black parents face that white parents do not. Black middle-class youth are not exempt from the same public abuse leveled against underclass black youth. They are racially profiled by police and anyone else who wants to target black youth. Therefore, working- and middle-class black parents have to teach their children what to do if they are stopped by the police while driving or walking. They are taught to make no sudden moves and to keep their hands visible; if stopped at night, turn the light on inside the car and do not argue with the police no matter how disrespectful they might be. Parents know their child—because of being black—could be shot to death, beaten, and arrested if he or she violates any of these rules.

In addition, underclass peers and whites who see no distinctions among blacks expect black middle-class youth to be sexually knowledgeable, experienced, and active. In the same way, black middle-class youth are expected to use, deal, and be knowledgeable about illegal drugs. A young black man who does not conform to these general social expectations could be labeled unmanly. A young black woman who fails the authentic code could be considered unattractive. Neither would be recognized as "black."

Parents have absolutely no room for error, and black youth have no time to mature or make mistakes in any social class. All normal and easy roads lead down to the underclass. There can be no idle television watching with televisions in their bedrooms—exposure to popular culture must be severely restricted. Every teacher must be investigated, met, monitored, and quickly switched if he or she cannot hold one's teens to high expectations. Peers must be sought who have parents practicing the same vigilance and restrictiveness, and closure must be around these peers. Any peer and parent in a young person's social network who is permissive and indulgent will be seen by one's own children as an ideal. This "ideal" will be held up against a more restrictive parent who can then be judged as draconian and the object of rebellion.

Not all black parents know to vigorously oppose popular culture. Most middle-class parents are from the working class and can tell you what it took for them to achieve upward mobility. But they do not know what it takes to socialize middle-class youth to remain in the middle class. They are learning as they go along, and there are no class-wide standards. By the time many realize what they are up against and understand what they must do to keep their children out of the underclass, it is too late. All it takes to fail for the long term are a couple of disapproving teachers, a brief period of identification with oppositional peers, one experiment with drugs, an encounter with the police, or sex with the wrong person.

For black parents to succeed with their children at home and in school is still not enough; there are the streets. Here again, most white middle-class parents do not live in neighborhoods that offer the same level of social and physical danger for themselves and their children as do black middle-class parents. The black middle class that lived in central cities in the 1960s became the targets of the crime that accompanied urban living and were forced out by drug trafficking. Analysis of where they moved shows that most got only as far as racial fringe urban neighborhoods that exist between the black working class (itself in meltdown) and the white lower-middle and working classes (Pattillo-McCoy, 1999). This is not far enough away from the black underclass and those who have been led to believe it is "black" to emulate that class. Black parents have much less control over who their young people choose to socialize with and encounter than do white parents. Gangs, drugs, sex, and violence are closer to black middle-class doorsteps than one thinks. Even if black parents do everything right at home and in school, they can still lose their young people to the streets.

In effect, it is more the exception than the rule for African American young people to remain in the middle classes or to be upwardly mobile from the underclass. Black parenting means having to engage in social and cultural guerrilla warfare twenty-four hours a day, seven days a week for twenty or more years against schools, peers, the media, the streets, police, and one's own children. The only black middle-class parents who have not faced these challenges and long odds have reared their children overseas, away from US culture, away from stereotyped racial expectations, lost peers, low expectations, the streets, and the pull of the fascination in the United States with the black underclass (Pattillo-McCoy, 1999; Snowden, 2002).

Other Vulnerabilities

Racial discrimination continues to make the black middle class vulnerable. As much as conservatives try to deny that discrimination exists, biographies and interviews of middle-class black Americans consistently report that they still experience racial discrimination (Collins, 1997; Cose, 1993; Feagin and Sikes, 1994; Fulwood, 1996). In fact, there have been indications since the 1960s that racial discrimination at work particularly targets middle-class blacks (Blau and Duncan, 1967; Feagin and Sikes, 1994), and although it is muted, such discrimination is equally pernicious in community life (Hartigan, 1999). White racism (the presumption of white racial superiority and the assumed right to be treated accordingly) is very much alive, well, and thriving. Blacks at high levels in US corporations report (privately) that they still are discriminated against by white peers at work (Collins, 1997; Jones, 1973, 1986; Zweigenhaft and Domhoff, 2003). Their intelligence, work ethic, preparation, judgment, and ability to lead whites especially are all in question, far beyond the extent that their white peers are questioned. In the academy, a white professor who publishes a book or paper is congratulated; when a black professor does the same, the accomplishment is more often ignored and minimized. In the corporate and academic worlds, whites are promoted in due course, sometimes—because of extenuating circumstances—even when they do not fully meet the standard. Blacks must be twice as qualified to demonstrate that they are only as qualified as whites for the same promotion. There are no extenuating circumstances for blacks; any shortcoming is grounds for disqualification, and if shortcomings do not exist, they can be found.

The reality is that blacks do not advance in any sector without strong backing from established whites who must literally block racially motivated attacks, questions, and anxieties from other white executives and faculty. Furthermore, it is naive to think that official criteria for promotion and retention are all one has to meet. Blacks who are successful in these worlds make few mistakes, and when they do, they do not make them twice. They also do not provide their white colleagues with personal reasons to question their work and presence. These are burdens that many white colleagues cannot begin to imagine as conditions for class membership.

Racism exists even in professional sports in which blacks appear to be well established. It is said that white athletes are brilliant and hard working, but blacks are said to be naturally athletic, to be not as smart, to perform inconsistently, and to be limited to roles "they" can play well (Bruce, 2004; Coventry, 2004). Black writers can only be angry, whereas white writers are allowed to express a full range of emotions. It is taken for granted that if you are black and enter any upscale store, security will watch your every move, and if it is a restaurant, an attempt will be made to seat you nearest the kitchen, reservations or not. There are companies to this day that have not hired any blacks as managers. There are also liberal arts and social-behavioral science departments at US universities and colleges that have never hired a black faculty member. These organizations claim that more than forty years after the Civil Rights Acts, they have been unable to find a single black who is qualified or who, if qualified, would come to their company or university. There are others that hired a black once some time ago, but because that person did not work out, they will never hire another. There are residential communities that blacks cannot buy into and social clubs that will find every reason not to admit blacks as members.

Continued racial discrimination is not simply a personal inconvenience and annoyance. In the workplace it is a real barrier to upward mobility and to a more secure position in the middle class. Discrimination in public accommodations is a reminder that many white Americans, consciously or not, still consider themselves superior to blacks and have the power to exercise this belief. Furthermore, if you are black, what are you going to do about it? Lawsuits cost money and time that one does not have.

Lack of an Upper Class

Blacks had no equivalent of the white upper class during the pre–World War II years, and one still does not exist. This is in fact the clearest indication of the historic impact of racism on African Americans. One might protest that, indeed, a class of wealthy African Americans now exists that did not prior to 1964. People such as Michael Jordan, Oprah Winfrey, and Bill Cosby certainly constitute an upper class. There were five black chief executive officers (CEOs) of Fortune 500 corporations in 2005 (Jones, 2005) and more than 200 others in striking distance of becoming CEOs in the future (Zweigenhaft and Domhoff, 2003). There are a legion of other highly paid business executives, professional athletes, actors, entertainers, television personalities, and rappers. They have money and lots of it. As we have already seen, the problem is that merely having money does not make someone upper class.

All contemporary, famous, and rich African Americans have one thing in common: they earned their money in their lifetime, and their professional position and status as celebrities cannot be passed on as an inheritance. Some may take great pride in coming from families that have had middle-class values for generations and for struggling to the top, but their success and money are still first generational (Benjamin, 1991; Edwards and Polite, 1992). Black women who have struggled into the middle class have a particular story to tell (Higginbothan, 2001). Black celebrities and executives clearly have enough money to carry wealth over into subsequent generations, but it remains to be seen whether they will succeed in doing so. To achieve the standard of "old money," their estates will have to carry on for at least two generations. At that point, they will have reached the minimum threshold for admission into the English American upper class of the United States. Catholic Irish Americans, after more than a century of economic mobility, have been well represented among corporate CEOs for years. They have barely made it in the upper class. There are Italian and Jewish Americans who are now in their third generation of wealth; they have not yet to crack open the door of the US upper class (Zweigenhaft and Domhoff, 1998).

The current generation of wealthy African Americans is not the first to try. At the turn of the twentieth century, Madam C. J. Walker was the wealthiest black woman of her time, owing to sales of her hair-care products. Her wealth, however, never made it past her grandchildren's generation (Lowry, 2003). Consider the first generation of wealthy black athletes and entertainers who integrated their respective fields— Joe Louis, Jackie Robinson, and Nat King Cole. They were better educated and prepared for their role than their contemporaries; but even though some of their descendants are well off, they cannot be compared to the Rockefellers, Danforths, Carnegies, or Crockers. Even the two African American families whose millions were gained in the prior generation through business are not there: the Johnson family of *Ebony* and

Jet magazines and the Johnson family of black hair-care products. All of these people are well off and successful, but they are not considered upper class by anyone other than blacks, the white middle class, and the media. Blacks who attended elite prep schools, colleges, and universities through the privately sponsored A Better Chance (ABC) and went onto corporate fast tracks at the very best time (the 1970s) were struggling in the early 1990s just to stay in the game (Zweigenhaft and Domhoff, 1991); this highly selective group had few children, and the ones they had are struggling just to stay in the middle class (Zweigenhaft and Domhoff, 2003). None of the ABC cases followed and interviewed by Zweigenhaft and Domhoff over the past thirty years is anywhere near cracking through to the US upper middle class.

One might think: who needs the old moneyed upper class with Oprah Winfrey's money? Wealthy African Americans should start their own "upper class." Well, this was done and long before Oprah. The children of the mulatto aristocracy, some of whom can date their family status back to the turn of the twentieth century, have maintained their tight-knit social networks and organization. Jack and Jill, Inc., is complete with its equivalent of the white upper class *Social Register,* called *Up the Hill,* a book members can use to look up other members to find and maintain association with "our kind of people." Even though the black self-defined "upper class" has neither real money nor power, its members do have a sense of longevity and exclusiveness, to quote Lawrence Graham:

> Bryant Gumbel is, but Bill Cosby isn't.
> Lena Horne is, but Whitney Houston isn't.
> Andrew Young is, but Jesse Jackson isn't.
> And neither is Maya Angelou, Alice
> Walker, Clarence Thomas, or Quincy Jones.
> And even though both of them try extremely
> Hard, neither Diana Ross nor Robin Givens
> Will ever be. (Graham, 1999:1)

Jack and Jill now admits brown-skinned African Americans if they are from prominent and wealthy black families who are without controversy and scandal (Graham, 1999). But this is still only a self-defined "upper class" status for blacks who would be considered at best upper middle class across the race line.

To think that blacks or any other ethnic group can become "upper class" simply because they have lots of money is to misunderstand power and influence in US life. The upper class of power and influence is not open to newcomers with just lots of money and celebrity status. The very rich and this nation's power elite are not necessarily the same people, but there is considerable overlap, now (Zweigenhaft and Domhoff, 1998) and in the past (Pessen, 1973, 1974). One can even have the values of the upper class and have gone to the right prep schools and universities. To maintain extraordinary and invisible power and influence over generations requires limiting the number of people involved. In effect, power must be monopolized and restricted. If "our kind of people" among blacks really wanted to be upper class, they would have to go up against the most prominent and most powerful white families in the nation for their control of the nation's primary institutions—banks, corporations, the United States Senate, and federal and state governments. Pretense would be no match for real power in a zero-sum game. A lot of new interlopers into the upper class would diminish the holdings of those who are already there. So newcomers who manage to hold on to their wealth for several generations are not going to be automatically admitted. In fact, upper class extended family members have no guarantee of class participation. The real struggle that the white upper class has is managing its wealth through the claims of vast networks of extended kin. There are now thousands of them who are middle class or less and who want to lay claim to vast old-money estates and assets.

Lacking a real black upper class means the black middle class has to fill in for missing elites in their civic and cultural lives. Black philanthropies and social services have a very limited network of wealthy blacks to whom to turn. Instead, they have only middle-class blacks who have little wealth and even limited incomes. In the black community, successful fund raising means thousands, not millions, of dollars. There are no blacks who can run for local and national political office and ease their way in by spending millions of their own dollars on their own political campaigns. Blacks cannot influence whoever is in office in Washington and in state governments through major campaign gifts and networks of donors. Furthermore, lack of an upper class means there is no group that is independently wealthy and that can devote itself to improving and leading the race. All blacks involved in social change and addressing the issues of the race first have to earn a living.

Lessons for the Mainstream Middle Class

The black middle class is virtually without wealth and depends totally on its income. It has few resources with which to shield itself from changes in the economy and larger society. It is therefore very vulnerable to short- and long-term trends in employment and social organization. It feels the economic breeze before the storm, unlike the white middle class, which does not feel the same storms until much later. In this regard, the twists and turns in the fate of the new black middle class tell us a great deal about subtle but important trends in US society as a whole.

The relationship between the black and white middle classes is analogous to the dynamics between long timers and first timers on a food-line. The long timers (black middle class) have learned how to live without, are on the "streets," are resigned to being dirty and viewed as undeserving and derelict—they are in the middle class owing to affirmative action. The newcomers (white middle class) are still in clean clothes, are down to their last fifty dollars, have no idea how they will survive once their money runs out, and are frightened to death of the reality of becoming like the long timers on the line. They are angry at what is happening to them and blame others all around them. Everyone knows who they are, but no one talks to them, and they are given lots of space because they can explode at any time on anyone around them.

This is the situation of the white US middle class and puts into context their emotional opposition to affirmative action and their attraction to regressive conservatism. Anyone who looks at the black middle class can see that its position has been and continues to be increasingly precarious. But the biggest secret in the United States today is that the white middle class is not too far behind, as suggested by Kevin Phillips (1993). Their days are numbered too. One only has to look at the condition of the black middle class, apart from the discrimination it faces, to see what the white middle class may soon face. The following sections discuss some well-advanced trends.

Decline of Enterprise as the Basis of the Middle Class

The middle class that Adam Smith, Max Weber, and Karl Marx examined was a class of small-business owners and entrepreneurs. Members earned their living by making, marketing, buying, and selling goods and services. It was a virtual religion to businessmen to have the freedom to do whatever they wanted and needed to do to make money. Governmental or religious interference through taxes and regulations was anathema. Some members of this class established themselves in new industries early enough to dominate them and to become exceedingly wealthy and influential: the Vanderbilts in railroads, the Carnegies in steel, and the Rockefellers in oil. This is the dream of all enterprising members of the middle and working classes. To gain great wealth is the essence of the "American dream" that existed long before the post–World War II middle class in the United States.

In the nineteenth century, 75 percent of the population consisted of farmers, businesspersons, and other entrepreneurs who were self-employed (Braverman, 1974). Very few of these people made sufficient money to even approach the lifestyle of the modern middle class. It was their independence, pride in ownership, and hard work that were most important to them. The idea of becoming independently wealthy was so strong that people who worked for others as clerks, accountants, foremen, and handymen, as well as those who were dissatisfied with their lot, jumped at opportunities to gain financial independence. The century-long rush to settle land in the US West, despite the "inconvenience" that the land belonged to the Native Americans, is an example. The 1849 California gold rush was a high point. But by 1870, with the onset of massive industrialization, self-employment had declined to 34 percent. By 1948, it was down to 18.5 percent, and by 2003 it stood at 7.5 percent (US Department of Labor, 2004). This history puts into perspective the problem of solving black economic subordination through entrepreneurship and self-help (Butler, 1991). This solution is 100 years too late and is like pushing the historical economic ball backwards and uphill.

Self-employment and entrepreneurship no longer reflect the current basis of the historic middle class. Instead, the majority of members of the US middle class are now employees. One might argue that a preponderance of businesses in the United States have fewer than fifty employees. This detail is always cited as evidence of continued enterprise and opportunity. But people fail to reveal that franchises and national and multinational corporations are eroding the financial and client base of independent small businesses. Consistent with historical trends, larger businesses can produce more goods and services at a lower cost to consumers. One only needs to look at shopping malls to see what corporate "anchor" and franchise stores are doing to small downtown retailers. The small businesses cannot compete with Sears, Macy's, and Nordstrom, and it is unknown how long even these large retail corporations will be able to compete with Wal-Mart and Costco. The white middle class is much more like the black middle class in its dependency than we realize. The bottom line is that increasingly both the black and white middle classes are employees in large organizations. The only structural difference is that the black middle class is more advanced in its dependency.

Declining Need for the US Middle Class

There is a second long-term trend that needs to be considered when people celebrate the existence of a majority middle class. That trend is a declining need for middle-class labor. In one industry after another, the managerial and technical evolution from automation in the 1950s to computerization in the 1990s is characterized by a reduced demand for labor and the extraction of greater efficiency from remaining employees (Oskerman, 2006). Production of tangible products, once the responsibility of individual craftsmen, has now been mechanized almost completely; skilled workers have been downgraded and their crafts all but eliminated. The black working class was affected by this trend first because blacks were the newest and most tenuous members of the working class. The elimination of their jobs through suburbanization and automation preceded the decline of the national working class through globalization. It is false to assume that the middle class is exempt from job loss through globalization and can maintain its size or continue growing to manage increasingly efficient workplaces. The middle class is experiencing something that is well advanced in the working class. Globalization of US middle class jobs may be now fully underway. English-speaking people in other parts of the world can do the same work more efficiently and for a lot less money.

Some would argue that the US middle class is necessary in order for US corporations to continue to be profitable and is the largest consumer market of those corporations. Two developments may make this wishful thinking. First, you cannot maintain the middle class and keep it as an engine of consumption if you continue to eliminate well-paying jobs. The US manufacturers eliminated 2.8 million jobs between 2000 and 2003 alone (Andrew, 2004). I would add that it is unlikely that these people went to equal or better-paying jobs in the service economy. Second, a large part of middle-class spending is on debt and credit and for necessities (Warren and Tyagi, 2003). The greatest potential for growth in consumerism and profits is now overseas. China and India alone have more than one-third of the world's population, and they are the high-growth consumer markets in the twenty-first century. Latin America also has enormous potential. Furthermore, profit margins are likely to be very thin in the United States relative to overseas in the long run. In that case, the potential for rapid growth in consumerism is very limited in the United States, and there is significant competition for the little growth that remains. Zero percent interest, as with US auto loans, and low-cost gasoline cannot last forever. Available space is limited to build many more McDonald's, and automakers can only sell so many cars. Future long-term profitability is overseas and is no longer dependent on US middle-class consumption.

Dependency on Social Policy

The black middle class is criticized for being a creation of government policy. It came into being both in 1866 and in 1964 as a result of federal social policy (Civil Rights Acts) and regulation (affirmative action). The black middle class has been sustained by federal policy and regulation. But this structural support is eroding. The initial national consensus that really opened doors is gone. In contrast, there is the traditional belief that the white middle class is built on enterprise and real work and is not based on government regulation and social policy. Conservatives argue that the large size and influence of government, high taxes, and government regulation of business are major burdens on the middle class. Without these barriers, they say, the middle class would grow in numbers and strength and prosper as never before.

Conservatives are horrified that African Americans became part of the middle class through government regulation. But if they took a hard look at the underpinnings of their own social class, they would see that whites are equally vulnerable. Although their dependency on government is not as advanced as it is for blacks, it is, in fact, increasing over time. Decreasing the size of the federal government in the face of corporations that are already larger than many world governments would have just the opposite impact. It would be the suicide of the middle class. The middle class in the United States is less and less the product of enterprise and self-initiative. It increasingly owes its existence to the very federal tax policies and regulation that conservatives want to eliminate.

If federal home mortgage interest deductions and business and charitable giving tax write-offs disappeared tomorrow, a sizable part of the white middle class would disappear as well. The middle class is an outcome of liberal federal home loan policies that openly discriminated against blacks until 1964 and continue to discriminate to this day, though more subtly (Phil, 2003; Ross and Yinger, 2002). A home is the largest asset for most members of the middle class, a home financed through government and private government-regulated loans. In addition, the middle class has yet to pay the full cost of transportation, a situation that has made it possible for its members to enjoy the suburban way of life ("Separate and Unequal," 2000). Public transportation for commuters to the suburbs is in fact subsidized by working-class people who use public transportation more frequently for shorter distances and during off-hours (Hanson, 1986). The middle class has enjoyed federally funded highways on which to drive to work, extraordinarily low gas prices compared to other parts of the world, and overdependence on private automobiles even though it has become clear that world oil supplies will not last forever. If and when these subsidies disappear, the US middle class will be reduced in size.

The point is that government regulation props up more than the black middle class; increasingly it is what sustains the white middle class as well. This is only half the story. The declining need for the US middle class at home points to its dependency on large multinational corporations. The extent to which these megacorporations and their subsidiaries want to employ Americans is another factor regulating the size of the US middle class. One must assume that Americans will continue to be needed as managers and sales staff at home. But the emerging middle classes in India, China, and Latin America will be the ones who will profit from the expansion of global economies. Their lower labor costs and multilingual skills alone make Americans noncompetitive overseas where the highest growth potential exists.

Rising Cost of Living

The African American working and middle classes had two generations of experience with working wives and mothers before white women had to go to work to maintain their families' standards of living and lifestyles. There is nothing in African American culture that inclined blacks to compromise the "man as bread-winner" ethos some fifty years before white women went to work in massive numbers after 1970. Black women went to work early in the 1900s for the reasons whites must do so now: they simply could not afford the cost of living without both adults working.

Instead of looking at the black experience in US society within its larger social and economic context, the press and many academic researchers have argued for decades that black families and, in particular, black women are at fault for racial inequality (Moynihan, 1965, 1986). But from 1945 to 1975, the cost of living was the number-one domestic problem as measured by the consumer price index (Zunz, Schoppa, and Hiwatari, 2002). Living expenses were increased further by the Organization of Petroleum Exporting Countries (OPEC) oil boycott in the mid-1970s, and the cost of living has continued to rise ever since. This has slowly eaten away at the middle class and has induced white families to seek second incomes to make ends meet. But this has not solved the problem. Changes in the economy and the high cost of living have made it more difficult for young adults to move out on their own, and increasingly their income is needed to make ends meet for their parents. These additional pressures have caused white divorce, separation, and never-married rates to start to climb and to differ little from those of blacks (Kposowa, 1998). This was unimagined in 1965. But there is no equivalent to Daniel Patrick Moynihan, who is charging that white women are the reason white families are coming apart. No discernible attention is being paid to the unraveling of white family life, nor is there any recognition that white families are about to take the same economic plunge as have blacks.

It is ironic that the social trends that produced and have sustained the black middle class are the same trends that sustain the white middle class. What happens to blacks now happens to whites later. And later may be closer than people think. These insights on the plight of the black middle class provide a window to the white future for anyone who cares to look. This chapter has outlined changes in the black middle class since the 1930s and found the same underlying dynamics at play for the white middle class. Black middle class "exceptionalism" and vulnerabilities are not so unique after all.

8

The Future of Race, Economic Inequality, and Class

It should be evident from the prior chapters that racial economic inequality in the United States has not really changed since 1940. A world war, a cold war, and a civil rights movement have come and gone. US society is affluent far beyond what could have been imagined in the 1950s. Now even the poor have color televisions and indoor plumbing, and many are obese from their consumption of fast food and their lack of exercise. For the first time in US history, a majority of Americans can really claim they are middle class. But despite the changes, black and white racial economic inequality persists, and race has far from declined in significance even for the middle class. The civil rights movement was very successful in eliminating the most obvious practices of racial supremacy, but dislodging racial economic inequality was beyond the scope of the movement.

Since 1964, racial poverty and overt discrimination have been replaced by benign neglect of the urban poor, deindustrialization, drug trafficking, commercialization of the underclass lifestyle, and a war on drugs that has criminalized one in three black males between eighteen and twenty-nine years of age ("Black Men and the Criminal Justice System," 1996). African Americans are in fact worse off economically and more vulnerable to downward mobility today than they were in 1965.

If the concept of socioeconomic status (SES) embraced family intergenerational human capital and assets, each black social class would be equivalent to the next *lower* white social class. It would also make it very clear that the black middle class overall cannot be compared to the white middle class. An immediate implication is that affirmative action has not produced a black middle class with any real advantages over whites in the same social class. Affirmative action has only helped to produce the appearance of racial interclass equality. When we consider that black social classes at the turn of the twenty-first century are in fact the equivalent of the next lower white social class, it is also clear that there is a great deal of myth and fiction about the contemporary black middle class.

Some Myths About the Black Middle Class

Much of the contemporary literature looks at the black middle class as if it has no history and no social context. Then myths replace reality. The myth of black middle-class comparability with the white middle class is the most important and strategic and was addressed in Chapter 5, but there are two others that need to be addressed.

Myth 1: The Middle Class Abandoned the Community

This myth is based upon the notion that the old black middle class lived and worked in the community with poor and working-class neighbors. They owned the stores and shops and were the dentists, doctors, teachers, and preachers. They could be seen going and coming from work and home; anyone who cared could observe and imitate their manners, disposition, dress, speech, and public habits. This myth asserts that since the 1964 Civil Rights Acts and housing desegregation, the new black middle class has moved into predominantly white communities and given up social ties in black communities. As a result, black communities have sunk into ghettos for lack of middle-class leadership and example. According to this myth, not only does the black middle class no longer live in the "hood," its members have given up doing business there as well. So the black poor have little day-to-day contact with the middle class other than as social service providers.

There are two problems with the myth of black middle class abandonment, problems with the facts and with the attribution of motives. In review, the fact is that most in the new black middle class have not moved very far from the "hood." There has not been a massive exodus of middle-class blacks from US cities to predominantly white suburbs. Most middle-class blacks live in communities near the ghetto. They live in areas generally bordered on one side by working- and lower-class black neighborhoods and on the other by working- and lower-middle class white communities (Pattillo-McCoy, 1999). Instead of being clustered within the black community, they are now clustered on its boundaries.

This clustering of the black "privileged" in edge communities is not a post-1965 development. A look at the long history of black communities in US cities since the founding of this nation shows that as cities have grown, blacks have progressively moved away from the downtown. For example, in the early 1700s, black slaves and freedmen lived near what is now Wall Street in New York City. A recently discovered black cemetery near the Stock Exchange and major federal buildings testifies to their presence on what was then the edge of the city (Brunius, 1999). In time, the black community moved farther up Manhattan Island to 14th Street, then to 34th Street, and then to 62nd Street, which was called San Juan Hill. As the value of the land increased and the downtown grew closer, blacks were pressured to move to cheaper land farther away. As a result, the next move for blacks was away from San Juan Hill and farther north to Harlem at the turn of the twentieth century (McKay, 1940). Each time the black community moved, the more prosperous served as the vanguard. This is precisely what is happening today all across the country.

Since 1960, the spatial center of the black community has shifted away from downtown toward the edges of the city and into the inner suburbs. Those who were better off have led the move as they have for more than 300 years. Southside Chicago started out as middle class, as did Compton, California, and Germantown in Philadelphia. West Oakland started as a refuge from the crowding and crime of San Francisco's black Fillmore district. In time, these middle-class residential areas passed on to the black working and lower classes. At one point, all three classes overlapped in the same general vicinity. So the "golden years" when all black social classes lived together have occurred more than once in the life histories of black communities. If the black middle class "abandoned" the black community in the 1970s, it was not the first time. The difference since 1965 has been that some members have been able to move farther away into predominantly white communities. But the majority could not and have not done so.

The myth of community abandonment deserves a few words on the topic of business abandonment. It is my contention that black men and women who bought small businesses from Jewish, Italian, and Irish immigrants during the 1950s ended up selling these businesses by the 1970s to new immigrants (Korean, Lebanese, etc.). In the face of rising unemployment, urban renewal, and declining earnings in rapidly evolving ghettos, black businesses were forced out. It became harder and harder to make a living, because national chain stores provided a greater variety of goods at lower prices with higher quality than neighborhood mom and pop stores could offer. This is still the case, even if the chain stores are not in the immediate neighborhood. Small family businesses declined in black communities for the same reason they declined in Main Street USA. They could not compete with larger (corporate) businesses with lower prices. Fast food franchises wiped out black restaurants and food stands. The few black entrepreneurs who were able to get some of these franchises have survived. But as the black working class was wiped out, only the black poor were left alone to support neighborhood businesses. In other words, the economic base in black neighborhoods after 1975 was insufficient to support a comprehensive small-business sector. There is an irony that Korean, Lebanese, and other ethnic businesses are in black communities. Foreign middle-man minorities survive in these businesses only by working after hours and weekends, living on the same premises as their businesses, and relying on unpaid extended family as labor. This is a point often ignored in the economics of ethnic enclaves (Li, 2000).

Another assumption of the abandonment myth is that the new black middle class does not want to live near the black working and lower classes. This applies particularly to those motivated to move into white communities to get away from other blacks. The real untold story is that most middle-class blacks left because of increasing drugs and crime—for the same reason whites had moved earlier. After 1965, rising unemployment led to drug trafficking. It was virtual suicide for anyone who was materially comfortable to remain in the community amid this broad heroin epidemic. Addicts have to finance their habits and are willing to use any means to get the necessary funds. Consequently, middle-class residents' homes were targeted first for break-ins. The middle class did not abandon black communities: most were driven out by an unprecedented wave of muggings, break-ins, and stickups committed by heroin addicts.

Myth 2: Low Marriage and High Separation Rates Constrain the Black Middle Class

The Moynihan thesis attributed black racial inequality to the lack of black family formation, and he believed that this situation was what social policy should have addressed in the 1960s (Moynihan, 1965). The Moynihan distortion of the work of one of the primary scholars of black family life, E. Franklin Frazier, went as follows: single or separated black men and women fail to improve their economic situation (that is, to attain middle-class income and status) because the black matriarchy places relationships with mothers and extended family ahead of relationships with spouses. Blaming black mothers for the absence of a strong middle class has been soundly repudiated (Bracey, Meier, and Rudwick, 1971; Tucker and Mitchell-Kernan, 1995). Other scholars also have attempted to correct Moynihan's theory of attribution (Rainwater and Yancey, 1967). In recent years, blacks' failure to marry and, therefore, to improve economically has been attributed to psychological and cultural causes rather than to a matriarchy. Economic and public policies solutions are no longer discussed (Collins, 1998). Holistic portrayals of black families that describe the circumstances of men and fathers in the lives of their children and mothers are also carefully avoided (Hill, 1998). The literature of modern psychology suggests that blacks are the cause of their own inequality: parents lack a belief in their "efficiency" with their children (Ardelt and Eccles, 2001), mothers are too poorly educated to be good parents (Jackson, 2003), or fathers and husbands have abandoned their wives and children and are not in the picture at all (Jackson, 2003).

Like the abandonment myth, on the surface the myth that the black family is responsible for continued racial inequality has some truth to it. The ability to afford a home and to have the lifestyle, quality of life, and consumption levels associated with the middle class are indeed increasingly dependent on two incomes. Loss of one income is disastrous if there are no other assets. When considering the failure of some blacks to marry, the new cultural and psychological explanations do not take into consideration that the plight of black women and children is impacted by the plight of many black men who are surviving outside of the US economy or at its edges. Decline in the incidence of intact marriages among blacks has been associated with the declining economic status of black men (Wilson, 1987). At minimum, having sufficient material resources is essential to forming and maintaining successful marriages. The lack of material resources suppresses marriage rates and undercuts existing marriages. This tendency has been documented in western European history going back to sixteenth-century England (Morris, 2005; Royle, 1997). Marriage, separation, and divorce do not happen solely based upon the moral character of a people. There are economic and material preconditions, a point that seems to be grasped for everyone except blacks.

Of course, there are people who have everything yet still separate and divorce for reasons of incompatibility, abuse, unhappiness, and so on. Not everyone, even in the middle class, is so materially secure, however, that they can have such noneconomic problems.

The late Daniel Patrick Moynihan could certainly have felt vindicated in the sense that he first called attention to the connection between weakness in black family formation and subsequent racial economic inequality. He had seen black family statistics and racial economic inequality get worse over a forty-year period (Moynihan, 1986). But the problem was that he still had the causal sequence wrong. (He tried unsuccessfully to get several prominent black scholars to support his position; they forewarned him of his misrepresentation [Lewis, 2002].) Over time, family structure responds to material conditions, not the other way around. What Moynihan should have noted in 1965 was that black economic status already had been dependent on two incomes for almost two generations. In 1965, one income in most white households was sufficient to support a family. This was before large numbers of white women found it necessary to go to work for the same reason black women went to work earlier—to maintain their middle-class status.

Black and White Future

It is easy to generate myths about a social class when one does not have the big picture. One thing this book attempts to do is to provide an overview of social class in US society and to show what black social classes illustrate about class. The social sciences gained importance prior to World War II largely because social scientists were able to provide the first convincing comprehensive picture of an evolving US society. Academic departments in colleges and universities were set up to advance this work (Platt, 1998; Wilson, 1968). Since World War II, social scientists in attempting to become more scientific have lost their mission to provide the big picture. As a consequence, the macroviews of US society have been obscure. We do not see the working parts, their interdependencies and functionalities.

Post–World War II studies and literature about the middle class cannot escape the fact that the middle class leads a very fragile existence. Historically, the class has come and gone. The contemporary US middle class faces the same possibility. The white and black middle classes walk a tightrope and can stay on it only under very specific circumstances. Changes in the overall middle class and its vulnerabilities are difficult to see amid almost two centuries of growth. In contrast, the black middle provides a picture of the overall middle class's limits and vulnerabilities. Two distinct black middle classes have come and gone since 1865. Today's black middle class is the third, may be the clearest mirror of trends in US society, and may be more fragile than its two predecessors. One important point mentioned in prior chapters needs to be repeated: that of the increasing dependency on business and government of the overall middle class.

Dependence on Business and Government

The future prospects for the lower ranks of the US middle class are apparent in what has happened to working- and lower-class blacks in the United States. The US public has yet to realize that the foundations on which the middle class is built have shifted from small-business enterprise to large corporate employers. In addition, the middle class has grown heavily dependent on the taxation and money management policies of the federal government. In the 1800s, small business was the ticket into the middle class and to personal independence, even if it was not the route to higher incomes. Now, however, more Americans are employees than ever before. Small businesses cannot compete against Wal-Mart–sized retailers, and big business is the most powerful institution in US life. This is a fact, regardless of one's personal ideology, and is acknowledged by conservatives and liberals alike.

The impact of sixty years of businesses shifting industries to the suburbs, into the South, and then overseas is most evident in the deindustrialized black working class. The result is an expanding underclass of people out of work, out of the economy, and effectively out of civil society. The existence and significance of this underclass has been ignored because of the token presence of the black middle class. By having a black middle class, there is the impression that all is normal and progressing well; the American dream exists—even for blacks. But hundreds of thousands of black laborers have been eliminated from the economy, and their plight has not been addressed. Instead, they and their children have been criminalized. If the "experiment" in downsizing employment has worked with blacks, it will certainly work for larger numbers of more privileged whites. If African Americans are the "canary" in the great US mine, then the same fate awaits white labor, but on a later timetable. Like that of their black counterparts, the downward social and economic mobility of whites is also obscured by the celebration of the white upper middle class (Brooks, 2000). In reality, there is an economic redistribution going on; the US working class is almost history, and we are witnessing the beginning of a declassing and deracing of the lower ranks of the white middle class as well.

Black laborers are vulnerable—not because of personal and moral deficiencies but because they are at the bottom of the labor market based on sixty years of Jim Crow racial segregation and 100 years of favoring European immigrants over English-speaking, readily available black labor. Furthermore, blacks are first into the underclass because of fifty years of benign neglect by federal social policies. Federal neglect of the increasingly desperate plight of blacks in the 1960s was reinforced by urban renewal and a war on drugs. Whole communities have been physically uprooted, destroyed as viable social entities, and then left to decline as social and economic entities until gentrification reclaims them for the middle class (Fullilove and Fullilove, 2000).

The contemporary black middle class is also a creation of federal policy—affirmative action—but the white middle class is increasingly dependent on federal policies as well. The size of the US middle class is also an outcome of federal subsidies in transportation, home and school loans, and tax breaks for retirement savings, mortgage payments, home offices, and personal business losses. If any of these subsidies were changed or eliminated, the size of the US middle class would be impacted, starting with the most vulnerable in the lower middle class. This shift from small business to dependency on large business and government might remain obscure and of little consequence if it were not for another development—the emergence of a global economy.

Who Needs the American Middle Class?

Globalization and the central role that US businesses play in it are accelerating the redefinition of the economic underpinnings of the US middle class. Ultimately, these changes will decide who will and will not be part of the middle class. In effect, the upper and upper middle classes' investment of US capital in the development of jobs in the Far East and in Latin and South America has all but wiped out the US working class, with the lower middle class close behind. The US lower middle class is now experiencing the same declassing, disciplining of wage demands, reorganization, and downsizing that the black working class underwent in the 1960s and 1970s. Virtually everyone in the lower middle class knows that they are increasingly vulnerable and have no long-term guarantee of employment at their current level.

Most Americans simply do not understand what is happening, or why, but they do know that their economic and personal circumstances, like those of the people around them, are threatened. The black middle class may be angry about continued racial discrimination and their inability to do anything about it, but the white lower middle class is angry for another reason: their social class status is eroding. If it is not immediately apparent in their lives, it certainly is apparent in their children's inability to get secure jobs, buy homes, or live comfortably on one income as their parents did at the same age and stage of life.

The Democratic Party has yet to recognize the extent of this anger and insecurity in the lower middle class. They make no promises to contain globalism. Instead, they argue that globalization is a good thing that will produce more jobs in the long run—for example, the North American Free Trade Agreement (NAFTA) in the Clinton administration. In addition, as whites are pushed out of the middle class, the only thing Democrats can offer them is the current welfare state, which is deeply offensive to an already insecure and fearful white middle class. Public housing, food stamps, and public education are all associated with the black poor or others who have been portrayed as "losers." For whites to be eliminated from the middle class is more than a personal failure; it is to drop to the level of blacks and other minorities; this is worse than being declassed. For whites it means losing one's higher-race status and social privileges as well.

Conservative Republicans better understand white fear of decline because they live with the same fear. They not only understand it; they have learned to exploit it. Although they will do no more than Democrats about globalization or seek to slow the decline of labor in the United States, at least they occasionally use antiglobal rhetoric. They also give the white lower middle class some hope about never having to face falling in class standing. They do so by promising to return the United States to the "greatness" of the 1950s by eliminating anything and everything associated with the welfare state. You cannot become part of a welfare state if it no longer exists. What is so ironic is that the conservatives' goal of reducing the size and influence of the federal government will only accelerate middle-class decline and their own class suicide. Big government in a global economy is necessary; their objective should be that government be more effective and efficient. While the white middle class is expressing its insecurity through a shift to conservatism, many in the black middle class are finding refuge in theologically conservative churches. As they and those around them descend economically, at least they will find refuge in the Lord. They know better than anyone else that to depend on the US welfare state is to be condemned to a living hell in this lifetime.

Whites think that the system is fair, except for reverse discrimination, and that racial discrimination was eliminated in the 1960s. In this context, affirmative action is an unfair advantage that guarantees the black presence in the middle class at the same time whites are being threatened and declassed. If blacks cannot make it on their own without a government crutch, then perhaps it is because they are intellectually and morally inferior after all. Blacks know that the system is not fair for them or for whites. They know whites have built-in advantages and that racial discrimination has not disappeared.

There is nothing to celebrate about the current trend toward "diversity" as a means of ensuring a continued black presence in the middle class because the diversity rationale asserts no commitment to reducing racial inequality. Diversity programs state no particular goals to increase black presence in colleges, universities, businesses, and government, nor do they show any need to address continued black underrepresentation in the professions and in work. Diversity unmasks a fundamental truth about past efforts to support a black middle class. To those in power, liberals and conservatives alike, the black middle class was necessary to prove that the United States had eliminated its embarrassing race problem. It was important to demonstrate that the black poor and underclass had an option—to enter the middle class if they chose to.

In effect, the larger purpose for creating a black middle class was based on symbolism and ideology in Cold War politics. But now the Cold War is over. The opinions of newly independent African and Asian leaders regarding race relations in the United States are unimportant. The Soviet threat and competition are gone, Africa is a mess, and China is absorbed in its own economic development. Who in the international community cares what race relations look like in the United States? There is no one out there pressuring the United States to feel embarrassed about racial inequality. So the external ideological need for a black middle class is gone. Within black communities, there are major impediments to the kind of black poor and underclass rioting or protesting of the 1960s. The police have become sufficiently trained, reinforced, and armed to put down any disturbance. So there is no need to buy out black protesters with "anti-poverty" efforts or to have a black middle class as a model for others to aspire to. Diversity will assure Americans that there will be an indefinite symbolic black presence in the middle class. If the white lower middle class drops from the middle class, they will be damned if they leave blacks "at the table" after they go down. Blacks, not whites, will continue to be the last hired and the first fired. This is the American way.

Conclusion: A New Perspective on the Black Middle Class

Can we infer from this viewpoint how we should think about the black middle class? For one thing, we can see that the fate of the black middle class is not distinct from that of other blacks (Durant and Louden, 1986). An emerging black underclass and a disappearing black working class impact the black middle class and affect its viability. Throughout history, the interests of the middle class as a self-proclaimed social entity have always conflicted with those of the working class or Marxist proletariat. But because race (the presumption of European supremacy over all peoples of color) is more important than class in the United States, the black middle class is unique. Its fate is intimately linked with that of all other blacks and ultimately with other people of color in the world community.

Next, strip away the symbolic importance of the black middle class to whites and to itself, and one finds that the black middle class actually does not reflect the modal circumstance of African Americans. The more accurate characterization of the basic condition of African Americans in the United States is that of the working class and the underclass. For the foreseeable future, most African Americans will find themselves in a declining working class and a rising underclass. There is little to keep a declassed black middle class from falling back into the working class. A drop from the middle class for many can easily be nonstop into the underclass. In comparison to a white middle-class fall, the fall of the black middle class might be a short drop economically, but a long one psychologically. This is what keeps black middle-class parents awake at night. If their children cannot resist the gangster rappers' definition of black culture, oppositional peers, rampant consumerism, and low academic expectations, their children's destination is the underclass. Middle-class parents cannot bequeath their children knowledge, values, and personal characteristics to stay in the middle class in the same way that they can hand down property.

The comedian Bill Cosby was correct to speak out openly about the failure of African Americans of all classes to actively critique and oppose the commercialization and glorification of black underclass behavior and culture. By their silence, blacks have empowered gangster rappers and their corporate record promoters to define what it means to be "black" in the United States. Their definition is straight from the old minstrel show—oversexed, funny, moody, dangerous, foul-mouthed, immoral, ignorant, and uncivilized. Fundamentally, gangster rappers do not embody the hip-hop movement. Rather, they are a perversion of it that could not exist if it were not for the financial backing and promotion of the recording industry. It is interesting that gangster rap's version of black life—guns, murder, drug dealing, hatred of women, materialism, and individuality—is straight from the world of crack cocaine traffickers. Seventy percent of the audience that spends billions of dollars on this music consists of thirteen- to nineteen-year-old white males purchasing gangster rap CDs in suburban record stores (Kleinfield, 2000; Negus, 1999). A broader black audience is not making gangster rappers and the corporate record companies wealthy.

Gangster rappers do not reflect black life, in general, or hip-hop, in particular. They are antiblack and antiwomen pornographers who are exploiting both white and black youth for the profit of record companies. Indeed, black youngsters who embrace gangster rap look, talk, and act like (as Cosby calls them) the race's "dirty linen" (Lee, 2004). They cannot succeed academically or enter and stay in the middle class with gangster rap behaviors and worldviews. A double misfortune is that black comedians and athletes have embraced the gangster rappers' style and language, further advancing their negative influence. But what the black debate on Cosby's comments misses is the white "dirty linen" that gangster rap also generates. They are white youth who now think it is their constitutional right to call black people "niggers" and women "bitches." These are epithets popularized by gangster rappers. In effect, foul-mouthed gangster rappers have become the new arbiters of what constitutes appropriate public discourse for all blacks (Kennedy, 2002).

Furthermore, African Americans need to rethink wealth. Most blacks, even those in the middle class, do not understand the difference between wealth and income. How the middle class handles inheritance is indicative of its real class roots. Some blacks are fortunate enough to have a home with a paid-off mortgage and perhaps some other real estate. But when these assets are inherited, they are routinely dissipated by division among heirs—a seemingly natural and fair thing to do. Then these life-long inherited savings are further depleted by division in the next generation or through family vacations and new cars. Instead, these once-in-a-lifetime assets should be set aside, invested, allowed to increase in value across generations, and managed by responsible executors who understand their goal—to advance family wealth for the next generations. This is done initially by setting up living trusts and by educating families so they understand that leaving assets to appreciate across generations is everyone's contribution to the family's future. In time, one's grandchildren will be able to access interest from the principle for their educations and down payments on homes. Anything short of this is not real wealth. There is no reason why the white upper class should have a monopoly on intergenerational wealth.

Blacks are up against the wall regardless of their social class. There is no large black working class to serve as the cornerstones of protest. The contemporary black middle class shows neither the interest nor the inclination to mobilize blacks as their predecessors did against Jim

Crow in the 1950s. If intergenerational unemployment, criminalization of black youth, AIDS, school failure, and the dismantling of affirmative action do not constitute an equal if not greater motive to mobilize, then what would? Certainly the present black middle class has far more human and financial resources than the middle- and working-class men and women who were the backbone of the civil rights movement in the 1950s and 1960s. Yet, there is virtually no organizing, militancy, or protests, and the few who are engaged get very little support. Civil rights gains, now taken for granted, cannot be sustained for very long without protest and political pressure. If the contemporary black middle class expects to survive, it must recognize the dilemma it and other blacks are in and act to resolve it.

There are members of the black middle class who realize that they must address self-defeating behaviors among the working class and the underclass; since the mid-1980s the middle class has been the only group among blacks with the human and material resources to do so (Durant, 1986). Members of the middle class are largely ineffective if they try to teach working- and lower-class blacks to be middle class. As we saw in Chapter 3, this approach is modeled on the missionary origins of the black educated class. The underlying assumption is, if you act with self-respect and are clean, decent, respectable, and moral, decent white people will treat you with respect. Eventually, there will be no reason for racism and segregation because of one's behavior. This theory is based, however, on an inaccurate belief that racial economic inequality is the result of blacks' inherent poor behavior and lack of morals. In contrast, the "dirty linen" that Cosby referred to is the outcome of what sociologists call structural arrangements—gross inequalities in work and pay, high unemployment, poor education, inadequate housing, government policies of benign neglect and criminalizing the poor blacks, and exploitation of blacks and black culture for private profit by corporations.

The black middle class can be instrumental in effectively "uplifting" the underclass only by addressing structural barriers. In fact, its fate is reliant upon it, another point Du Bois made repeatedly (Gaines, 1996). There are three conditions that must be met to provide a powerful antidote to the social illness that produces any race's "dirty linen": (1) jobs that pay a living wage, (2) day-to-day freedom from threats and violence coming from drug dealers and police alike, and (3) a high-quality education that is more than a demonstration of high test scores. The first two conditions are part of the five prerequisites for developing a middle class. Anything less contributes to blacks' decline and does nothing to change the basis of black marginality. With work that pays a living wage, an education that challenges people to achieve their potential, and an environment minus daily threats, the black working class could be reconstituted, the underclass could be reduced in size, and blacks would be able to reaffirm and enforce conventional social norms and moral values.

Finally, if and when a critical mass in the black middle class does choose to act on structural issues rather than their symptoms, addressing racial inequality will be unavoidable and a new approach will have to be forged. The next movement cannot eliminate racial economic inequality through civil rights reforms aimed at helping just blacks and other racial minorities. Blacks cannot gain economic equality with whites or be given what white Americans do not have for themselves. Blacks cannot achieve economic equity if whites do not enjoy it too. The next movement has to attack the fundamental structure of economic inequality in US society. Doing this will make it possible to eliminate racial economic inequality. Only then will the larger society escape the fate of the black social class pyramid. Without a universal approach, there can be no long-term improvement in anyone's comparative economic position.

The white upper class is celebrating record increases in its fortune. The white upper middle class thinks it is in control and does not know what to do with all its income (Brooks, 2000). The white lower middle class has mounting anxieties about its future and is growing increasingly desperate and conservative. Its members are becoming more and more reactionary, reflecting the extent to which the interests of the white lower middle class conflict with those of the upper class. But all of this is obscured by their shared whiteness. Much could be done to prevent white declassing, but it would require an awareness of their class interests and a recognition that any downgrade in class is an outcome of decisions made to promote the interests of the white upper and upper-middle classes. Affirmative action and the presence of blacks and other people of color are not the cause of white insecurity and decline. The white lower-middle class, in fact, has more in common with blacks and people of color than its members have with white owners (upper class), managers, and publicists (upper-middle class).

Toward a Solution?

If globalization is the future, then solutions have to be global in perspective. This means the government has to find ways to integrate as many people as possible into this new economy, just as it did during the Great Depression. At minimum, this would require absolute reduction in the national debt, long-term and deep investment in education (rather than the kind of disinvestment that is occurring now), and an opportunity for everyone who can work to find jobs that pay living wages.

This would require terminating the costly, racist, and ineffective drug war by identifying those responsible for drug trafficking and stopping them. Then we could drastically reduce the size of the massive, expensive, and economically unproductive prison and criminal justice systems. It is cheaper, far more humane, and in the best interest of society overall for anyone who can work to have a job and to earn a living wage. If business alone cannot generate a sufficient number of entry-level jobs, then the federal government should subsidize the additional work. We either provide work that includes people in society and allows them to take care of themselves, or we pay higher costs for the criminal justice, health care, and related services that the underclass ends up consuming. As a society, we need to do just the opposite of what conservatives are calling for. But note that the solutions posed here do not constitute a continuation of the liberal welfare state where people are bought off and a whole class of able-bodied Americans is left with no meaningful role in the economy. Rather, the goal is to get everyone engaged in the economy so that no one is outside of society.

The black middle class is in the same position as the white lower-middle class. For blacks there is no whiteness to obscure an awareness of their own economic interests. Blacks have another problem. Racial consciousness disposes a very narrow view of self-interests; black Americans believe that their problems are limited to blacks. They therefore want to eliminate racial inequality and racial discrimination, but they have not taken into account what this achievement would mean for the larger society. Strategically, a single group cannot expect to succeed if the same opportunities do not exist in the larger society. In reality, the most effective racial liberation effort would require mitigating inequality for everyone in US society. This does not mean more affirmative action for blacks but rather social welfare policies that feature universal as opposed to race- and group-specific strategies (Wilson, 1987).

Real liberation also requires recognizing that the black middle class is not what it is purported to be—comparable to the white middle class and with the same interests. The black middle class cannot be compared with the white upper-middle class, which would go on celebrating its self-importance long after the black middle class had disappeared. In the end, black liberation is US liberation. Nothing will change until the historic stranglehold of injustice is broken for blacks and whites alike.

Appendix

Figure 5.2 Relationships Among Factors Influencing SES, White Respondents

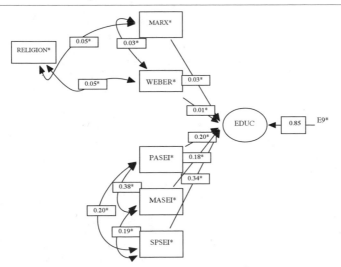

Notes: EQS: Chi Sq. = 12.70, P = 0.24, CFI = 0.99, RMSEA = 0.02

**Figure 5.3   Relationships Among Factors Influencing SES,
Black Respondents**

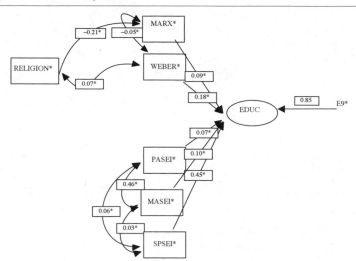

Notes: EQS 6: Chi Sq. = 11.87, P = 0.29, CFI = 0.95

Bibliography

Aldrich, N. W. (1988). *Old Money: The Mythology of America's Upper Class.* New York: Knopf.

Allen, T. (1994). *The Invention of the White Race: Racial Oppression and Social Control.* New York: Verso.

Althusser, L. (1969). *For Marx* (B. Brewster, Trans.). New York: Pantheon Books.

———. (1990). "Marxism Today." In G. Elliott (Ed.), *Philosophy and the Spontaneous Philosophy of the Scientists and Other Essays* (pp. 267–280). London: Verso.

Alvarez, R. M., García-Bedolla, L. (2004). "The Revolution Against Affirmative Action in California: Racism, Economics, and Proposition 209." *State Politics and Policy Quarterly 4*(1), 1–17.

Andrews, E. (2004). "The Jobless Recovery." *New York Times,* January 4, BU2, 7.

Anderson, E., Massey, D. (Eds.). (2001). *Problem of the Century: Racial Stratification in the United States.* New York: Russell Sage Foundation.

Aptheker, H. (1971). "Slave Resistance in the United States." In N. Huggins, M. Kilson, and D. Fox (Eds.), *Key Issues in the Afro-American Experience* (vol. 1, pp. 161–173). New York: Harcourt Brace Jovanovich.

———. (1983). *American Negro Slave Revolts.* New York: International Publishers.

Ardelt, M., Eccles, J. (2001). "Effects of Mothers' Parental Efficacy Beliefs and Promotive Parenting Strategies on Inner-City Youth." *Journal of Family Issues 22*(8), 944–973.

Asumah, S. N., Perkins, V. C. (2000). "Black Conservatism and the Social Problems in Black America: Ideological Cul-de-Sacs." *Journal of Black Studies 31*(1), 51–74.

Avery, R. B., Rendall, M. S. (2002). "Lifetime Inheritances of Three Generations of Whites and Blacks." *American Journal of Sociology 107*(5), 1300–1347.

Baltzell, E. D. (1958). *Philadelphia Gentlemen: The Making of a National Upper Class*. Glencoe, Ill.: Free Press.

———. (1962). *An American Business Aristocracy*. New York: Collier Books.

Baritz, L. (1989). *The Good Life: The Meaning of Success for the American Middle Class*. New York: Knopf.

Barnes, A. S. (2000). *Say It Loud: Middle-Class Blacks Talk About Racism and What to Do About It*. Cleveland, Ohio: Pilgrim Press.

Benjamin, L. (1991). *The Black Elite: Facing the Color Line in the Twilight of the Twentieth Century*. Chicago: Nelson-Hall Publishers.

Bennett, J. L. (1969). *Black Power USA: The Human Side of Reconstruction, 1867–1877*. Baltimore, Md.: Penguin Books.

Billingsley, A. (1992). *Climbing Jacob's Ladder: The Enduring Legacy of African-American Families*. New York: Simon and Schuster.

"Black Men and the Criminal Justice System." (1966). *Society 33*(5), 3–5.

Blackwell, J. (1987). *Mainstreaming Outsiders: The Production of Black Professionals*. Dix Halls, N.Y.: General Hall.

Blassingame, J. (1972). *The Slave Community: Plantation Life in the Antebellum South*. New York: Oxford University Press.

Blau, F. D., Graham, J. (1990). "Black-White Differences in Wealth and Asset Composition." *Quarterly Journal of Economics 105*(2), 321–339.

Blau, P., Duncan, O. (1967). *The American Occupational Structure*. New York: Wiley.

Bluestone, B., Harrison, B. (1982). *The Deindustrialization of America*. New York: Basic Books.

Blumin, S. (1989). *The Emergence of the Middle Class: Social Experience in the American City, 1760–1900*. New York: Cambridge University Press.

Boissonnade, P. (1964). *Life and Work in Medieval Europe: The Evolution of Medieval Economy from the Fifth to the Fifteenth Century* (E. Power, Trans.). New York: Harper and Row.

Boris, E. (1998). "Fair Employment and the Origins of Affirmative Action in the 1940s." *NWSA Journal 10*(3), 142–152.

Boskin, J. (1986). *Sambo: The Rise and Demise of an American Jester*. New York: Oxford University Press.

Bourgois, P. (1995). *In Respect: Selling Crack in El Barrio*. New York: Cambridge University Press.

Bowser, B. (1989). "Generational Effects: The Impact of Culture, Economy, and Community Across the Generations." In R. Jones (Ed.), *Black Adult Development and Aging* (pp. 3–30). Richmond, Calif.: Cobb and Henry.

———. (2002). "Studies of the African Diaspora: The Work and Reflections of St. Clair Drake." In B. Bowser and L. Kushnick (Eds.), *Against the Odds: Scholars Who Challenged Race in the Twentieth Century* (pp. 86–110). Amherst: University of Massachusetts Press.

Bowser, B., Hunt, R. (Eds.). (1996). *Impacts of Racism on White Americans*. 2nd ed. Thousand Oaks, Calif.: Sage Publications.

Bracey, J., Meier, A., Rudwick, E. (Eds.). (1971). *Black Matriarchy: Myth or Reality?* Belmont, Calif.: Wadsworth Publishing.

Branch, T. (1989). *Parting the Waters: America in the King Years.* New York: Simon and Schuster.

Braverman, H. (1974). *Labor and Monopoly Capital: The Degradation of Work in the Twentieth Century.* New York: Monthly Review Press.

Brooks, D. (2000). *Bobos in Paradise: The New Upper Class and How They Got There.* New York: Simon and Schuster.

Brooks, R. (1990). *Rethinking the American Race Problem.* Berkeley: University of California Press.

Bruce, T. (2004). "Marking the Boundaries of the 'Normal' in Televised Sports: The Play-by-Play of Race." *Media, Culture and Society 26*(6), 861–880.

Brunius, H. (1999). "African Burial Ground Under New York Streets." *Christian Science Monitor 91*, 141.

Butler, J. (1991). *Entrepreneurship and Self-Help Among Black Americans: A Reconsideration of Race and Economics.* Albany: State University of New York Press.

Cagetti, M., Nardi, M. (2005). "Wealth Inequality: Data and Models." Working paper WP 2005-10, Federal Reserve Bank of Chicago. www.chicagofed .org/publications/workingpapers/wp2005_10.pdf.

Cantor, M. (1970). *Black Labor in America.* Westport, Conn.: Negro University Press.

Caro, R. (1990). *The Years of Lyndon Johnson: The Path to Power.* New York: Knopf.

Cecil-Fronsman, B. (1992). *Common Whites: Class and Culture in Antebellum North Carolina.* Lexington: University Press of Kentucky.

Cell, J. W. (1982). *The Highest Stage of White Supremacy: The Origins of Segregation in South Africa and the American South.* New York: Oxford University Press.

Centers, R. (1961). The *Psychology of Social Class.* New York: Russell and Russell.

Chang, J. (2005). *Can't Stop, Won't Stop: A History of the Hip-Hop Generation.* New York: St. Martin's Press.

Chinoy, E. (1950). "Research on Social Structure." *Canadian Journal of Economics and Political Science 16*, 180–186.

Chiteji, N., Stafford, F. (1999). "Portfolio Choices of Parents and Their Children as Young Adults: Asset Accumulation by African-American Families." *American Economic Review 89*(2), 377–380.

Christopher, R. (1989). *Crashing the Gates: The De-WASPing of America's Power Elite.* New York: Simon and Schuster.

Churchill, W., Vander Wall, J. (1990). *The COINTELPRO Papers: Documents from the FBI Secret Wars Against Domestic Dissent.* Boston: South End Press.

Clark, W. (2003). *Immigrants and the American Dream: Remaking the Middle Class.* New York: Guilford Press.

Cohodas, N. (1993). *Strom Thurmond and the Politics of Southern Change.* New York: Simon and Schuster.

Collins, P. H. (1998). "Intersections of Race, Class, Gender, and Nation: Some Implications for Black Family Studies." *Journal of Comparative Family Studies 29*(1), 27–35.

Collins, S. (1997). *Black Corporate Executives: The Making and Breaking of a Black Middle Class*. Philadelphia: Temple University Press.

Cose, E. (1993). *The Rage of a Privileged Class*. New York: HarperCollins.

Coventry, B. T. (2004). "On the Sidelines: Sex and Racial Segregation in Television Sports Broadcasting." *Sociology of Sport Journal 21*(3), 322–342.

Cowie, J. (2002). "Nixon's Class Struggle: Romancing the New Right Worker, 1969–1973." *Labor History 45*, 257–283.

Cox, O. (1948). *Caste, Class and Race*. New York: Monthly Review Press.

———. (1964). *Capitalism as a System*. New York: Monthly Review Press.

Cromwell, A. M. (1994). *The Other Brahmins: Boston's Black Upper Class, 1750–1950*. Fayetteville: University of Arkansas Press.

Curtin, P. (1969). *The Atlantic Slave Trade: A Census*. Madison: University of Wisconsin Press.

Dalfiume, R. M. (1969). *Desegregation of the U.S. Armed Forces: Fighting on Two Fronts, 1939–1953*. Columbia: University of Missouri Press.

Daniels, J. (1914). *In Freedom's Birthplace*. New York: Houghton Mifflin.

Darrough, M., Blank, R. (1983). *Biological Differences and Social Equality: Implications for Social Policy*. Westport, Conn.: Greenwood Press.

Davidson, B. (1961). *The African Slave Trade*. Boston: Little, Brown.

Davies, G. (1996). *From Opportunity to Entitlement: The Transformation and Decline of Great Society Liberalism*. Lawrence: University Press of Kansas.

D'Emilio, J. (2003). *Lost Prophet: The Life and Times of Bayard Rustin*. New York: Free Press.

Dennis, R. (Ed.). (1995). *The Black Middle Class*. Greenwich, Conn.: JAI Press.

Dent, D. J. (2000). *In Search of Black America: Discovering the African-American Dream*. New York: Simon and Schuster.

Dillon, M. (1990). *Slavery Attacked: Southern Slaves and Their Allies, 1619–1865*. Baton Rouge: Louisiana State University Press.

Dollard, J. (1937). *Caste and Class in a Southern Town*. New Haven, Conn.: Yale University Press.

Domhoff, G. W. (1974). *The Bohemian Grove and Other Retreats: A Study in Ruling-Class Cohesiveness*. New York: Harper and Row.

Drake, S. C., Cayton, H. (1945). *Black Metropolis*. New York: Harcourt, Brace and Company.

Du Bois, W.E.B. (1903). *The Souls of Black Folks: Essays and Sketches*. Repr., New York: Blue Heron Press, 1953.

———. (1935). *Black Reconstruction in America, 1860–1880*. New York: Free Press.

———. (1945). *Color, Democracy: Colonies and Peace*. New York: Harcourt, Brace.

———. (1967). *The Philadelphia Negro*. New York: Schocken Books.

———. (1971). *The Negro*. London: Oxford University Press.

Dudziak, M. (2000). *Cold War Civil Rights: Race and the Image of American Democracy*. Princeton, N.J.: Princeton University Press.

Durant, T., Louden, J. (1986). "The Black Middle Class in America: Historical and Contemporary Perspectives." *Phylon 47*(4), 253–263.

Durr, K. D. (2003). *Behind the Backlash: White Working Class Politics in Baltimore. 1940–1980*. Chapel Hill: University of North Carolina Press.

Edsall, T. B. (1992). *Chain Reaction: The Impact of Race, Rights, and Taxes on American Politics*. New York: Norton.

Edwards, A., Polite, C. (1992). *Children of the Dream: The Psychology of Black Success*. New York: Doubleday.

Elliott, B., McCrone, D. (1987). "Class, Culture and Morality: A Sociological Analysis of Neo-Conservatism." *Sociological Review 35*(3), 485–516.

Esslinger, D. (1975). *Immigrants and the City: Ethnicity and Mobility in a Nineteenth Century Midwestern Community*. Washington, N.Y.: Kennikat Press.

Feagin, J. R., Sikes, M. (1994). *Living with Racism: The Black Middle-Class Experience*. Boston: Beacon Press.

Fein, R. (1966). *An Economic and Social Profile of the Negro American*. Washington, D.C.: Brookings Institute.

Finkle, L. (1975). *Forum for Protest: The Black Press During World War II*. Rutherford, N.J.: Fairleigh Dickinson University Press.

Fligstein, N. (1981). *Going North: Migration of Blacks and Whites from the South, 1900–1950*. New York: Academic Press.

Foner, E. (1983). *Nothing but Freedom: Emancipation and Its Legacy*. Baton Rouge: Louisiana State University Press.

Foner, P. (1962). *History of the Labor Movement in the United States*. New York: International Publishers.

Formisano, R. P. (2004). *Boston Against Busing: Race, Class, and Ethnicity in the 1960s and 1970s*. Chapel Hill: University of North Carolina Press.

Fraser, S. (Ed.). (1995). *The Bell Curve Wars: Race, Intelligence and the Future of America*. New York: Basic Books.

Frazier, E. F. (1957). *Black Bourgeoisie: The Rise of a New Middle Class*. New York: Free Press.

Fredrickson, G. (1971). *The Black Image in the White Mind*. New York: Harper and Row.

Freeman, J. B. (2000). *Working-Class New York: Life and Labor Since World War II*. New York: New Press.

Freeman, R. (1976). *The Black Elite: The New Market for Highly Educated Black Americans*. New York: McGraw Hill.

Fullilove, M. T., Fullilove III, R. E. (2000). "What's Housing Got to Do with It?" *American Journal of Public Health 90*(2), 183–185.

Fulwood, S. (1996). *Waking from the Dream: My Life in the Black Middle Class*. New York: Anchor Books.

Gaines, K. (1996). *Uplifting the Race: Black Leadership, Politics, and Culture in the Twentieth Century*. Chapel Hill: University of North Carolina Press.

Glasgow, D. (1980). *The Black Underclass: Poverty, Unemployment, and Entrapment of Ghetto Youth*. San Francisco: Jossey-Bass.

Glassman, R. (2000). *Caring Capitalism: A New Middle-Class Base for the Welfare State.* New York: St. Martin's Press.

Glenn, N. D. (1963). "Negro Prestige Criteria: A Case Study in the Bases of Prestige." *American Journal of Sociology 68,* 645–657.

Gordon, A. (1929). *Sketches of Negro Life and History in South Carolina.* Columbia: University of South Carolina Press.

Gordon, M. (1949). "Social Class in American Sociology." *American Journal of Sociology 55,* 262–268.

——. (1963). *Social Class in American Sociology.* New York: McGraw Hill.

Gordon, R., Rudert, E. (1979). "Bad News Concerning IQ Tests." *Sociology of Education 52*(3), 174–191.

Graham, A. (2003). *Framing the South: Hollywood, Television and Race During the Civil Rights Struggle.* Baltimore, Md.: Johns Hopkins University Press.

Graham, H. D. (1990). *The Civil Rights Era: Origin and Development of National Policy, 1960–1972.* New York: Oxford University Press.

Graham, L. (1999). *Our Kind of People: Inside America's Black Upper Class.* New York: HarperCollins.

Grayson, H. (1955). *The Crisis of the Middle Class.* New York: Rhinehart.

Grier, K. (1988). *Culture and Comfort: Parlor Making and Middle-Class Identity, 1850–1930.* Washington, D.C.: Smithsonian Institution Press.

Griffin, L. J., Evenson, R. J., Thompson, A. B. (2005). "Southerners All?" *Southern Culture 11*(1), 6–26.

Gross, L. (1908). "The Use of Class Concepts in Sociological Research." *American Journal of Sociology 14,* 409–421.

Guinier, L. (2005). "The Miner's Canary." *Liberal Education 91*(2), 26–31.

Gullickson, A. (2005). "The Significance of Color Declines: A Re-Analysis of Skin Tone Differentials in Post–Civil Rights America." *Social Forces 84* (1), 157–180.

Guttman, H. (1976). *Black Families in Slavery and Freedom, 1750–1925.* New York: Pantheon Books.

Hall, R. E. (2004). "Entitlement Disorder." *Journal of Black Studies 34*(4), 562–580.

Hamilton, R. F., Form, W. H. (2003). "Categorical Usages and Complex Realities: Race, Ethnicity, and Religion in the United States." *Social Forces 81*(3), 693–715.

Hanson, S. (Ed.). (1986). *The Geography of Urban Transportation.* New York: Guilford Press.

Hartigan, J. (1999). *Racial Situations: Class Predicaments of Whiteness in Detroit.* Princeton, N.J.: Princeton University Press.

Hechter, M. (1975). *Internal Colonialism: The Celtic Fringe in British National Development, 1536–1966.* London: Routledge and Kegan Paul.

Higginbothan, E. (2001). *Too Much to Ask: Black Women in the Era of Integration.* Chapel Hill: University of North Carolina Press.

Hill, M. E. (2000). "Color Differences in the Socioeconomic Status of African American Men: Results of a Longitudinal Study." *Social Forces 78,* 1437–1460.

Hill, R. (1998). "Understanding Black Family Functioning: A Holistic Perspective." *Journal of Comparative Family Studies 29*(1), 15–26.

Hilton, R. (1985). *Class Conflict and the Crisis of Feudalism: Essays in Medieval Social History*. London: Hambledon Press.

Holt, T. (1977). *Black over White: Negro Political Leadership in South Carolina During Reconstruction*. Urbana: University of Illinois Press.

House, F. (1934). "Measurement in Sociology." *American Journal of Sociology 40*(1), 1–11.

Howe, C. (1992). *Political Ideology and Class Formation: A Study of the Middle Class*. Westport, Conn.: Praeger.

Hunt, M. R. (1996). *The Middling Sort: Commerce, Gender, and the Family in England, 1680–1780*. Berkeley: University of California Press.

Hurley, A. (2001). *Diners, Bowling Alleys, and Trailer Parks: Chasing the American Dream in Postwar Consumer Culture*. New York: Basic Books.

Ignatiev, N. (1995). *How the Irish Became White*. New York: Routledge.

Jackson, A. P. (2003). "The Effects of Family and Neighborhood Characteristics on the Behavioral and Cognitive Development of Poor Black Children: A Longitudinal Study." *American Journal of Community Psychology 32*(1/2), 175–187.

Jaynes, G., Williams Jr., R. W. (1989). *A Common Destiny: Blacks and American Society*. Washington, D.C.: National Academic Press.

Jencks, C., Phillips, M. (Eds.). (1998). *The Black-White Test Score Gap*. Washington, D.C.: Brookings Institution Press.

Jernegan, M. W. (1965). *Laboring and Dependent Classes in Colonial America, 1607–1783*. New York: Frederick Ungar Publishing.

Johnson, M., Roark, J. (1984). *Black Masters: A Free Family of Color in the Old South*. New York: Norton.

Jones, D. (2005). "Companies with Black CEOs." *USA Today,* March 7.

Jones, E. (1973). "What's It Like to Be a Black Manager?" *Harvard Business Review 51*(4), 108–116.

———. (1986). "Black Managers: The Dream Deferred." *Harvard Business Review 86*(3), 84–93.

Kalmijn, M. (1996). "The Socioeconomic Assimilation of Caribbean American Blacks." *Social Forces 74*(3), 911–931.

Keister, L. A. (2000). "Race and Wealth Inequality: The Impact of Racial Differences in Asset Ownership on the Distribution of Household Wealth." *Social Science Research 29*(4), 477–503.

Keith, V. M., Herring, C. (1991). "Skin Tone and Stratification in the Black Community." *American Journal of Sociology, 97*(3), 760–779.

Kellenbenz, H. (1976). *The Rise of the European Economy: An Economic History of Continental Europe from the Fifteenth to the Eighteenth Century*. London: Weidenfeld and Nicolson.

Kelley, R. D. (1990). *Hammer and Hoe: Alabama Communists During the Great Depression*. Chapel Hill: University of North Carolina Press.

Kennedy, R. (2002). *Nigger: The Strange Career of a Troublesome Word*. New York: Pantheon Press.

Kerner, O., et al. (1968). *Kerner Commission Report*. New York: Dutton.

Kleinfield, N. R. (2000). "Guarding the Borders of the Hip Hop Nation." *New York Times,* July 6.

Kohn, M. (1969). *Class and Conformity: A Study in Values.* Homewood, Ill.: Dorsey Press.

Korzenny, F., Ting-Toomey, S. (Eds.). (1992). *Mass Media Effects Across Cultures.* Newbury Park, Calif.: Sage.

Kotlowski, D. J. (1998). "Richard Nixon and the Origins of Affirmative Action." *Historian 60*(3), 523–542.

Kposowa, A. (1998). "The Impact of Race on Divorce in the United States." *Journal of Comparative Family Studies 29*(3), 529–548.

Kriedte, P. (1983). *Peasants, Landlords, and Merchant Capitalists: Europe and the World Economy, 1500–1800.* Leamington Spa, Warwickshire: Berg Publishers.

Kuhl, S. (1994). *The Nazi Connection, Eugenics, American Racism, and German National Socialism.* New York: Oxford University Press.

Landry, B. (1978). "A Reinterpretation of the Writings of Frazier on the Black Middle Class." *Social Problems 26*(2), 211–222.

———. (1980). "The Social and Economic Adequacy of the Black Middle Class." In J. Washington (Ed.), *Dilemma of the New Black Middle Class* (pp. 1–14). Philadelphia: University of Pennsylvania's Afro-American Studies Program.

———. (1987). *The New Black Middle Class.* Berkeley: University of California Press.

Lee, L. (2004). "Cosby Defends His Remarks About Poor Blacks' Values." *New York Times,* May 22, B7.

Lewis, H. (2002). "Pursuing Fieldwork in African American Communities: Some Personal Reflections of Hylan Lewis." In B. Bowser and L. Kushnick (Eds.), *Against the Odds: Scholars Who Challenged Race in the Twentieth Century* (pp. 123–146). Amherst: University of Massachusetts Press.

Li, P. S. (2000). "Economic Returns of Immigrants' Self-Employment." *Canadian Journal of Sociology 25*(1), 1–34.

Litwack, L. F. (2000). "Hellhounds." In J. Allen, A. Hilton (Eds.), *Without Sanctuary: Lynching Photography in America* (pp. 8–37). Santa Fe, N.M.: Twin Palms Publishers.

Lloyd-Jones, R., Lewis, M. J. (1988). *Manchester and the Age of the Factory: The Business Structure of Cottonopolis in the Industrial Revolution.* London: Croom Helm.

Lorini, A. (1999). *Rituals of Race: American Public Culture and the Search for Racial Democracy.* Charlottesville: University Press of Virginia.

Lowry, B. (2003). *Her Dream of Dreams: The Rise and Triumph of Madam C. J. Walker.* New York: Knopf.

Lynch, F. R. (2005). "Corporate Diversity." *Society 42*(3), 40–48.

Lynd, R., Lynd, H. (1929). *Middletown.* New York: Harcourt, Brace.

———. (1937). *Middletown in Transition.* New York: Harcourt, Brace.

Martin, C. H. (1976). *The Angelo Herndon Case and Southern Justice.* Baton Rouge: Louisiana State University Press.

Marx, K. (1967). *Capital.* New York: International Publishers.

————. (1982). *The Marxist Reader.* New York: Avenel Books.

Marx, K., Engels, F. (1961). *Marx and Engels: Selected Correspondence.* London: Lawrence and Wishart.

Massey, D., Denton, N. (1993). *American Apartheid: Segregation and the Making of the Underclass.* Cambridge: Harvard University Press.

McBride, D., Little, M. (1981). "The Afro-American Elite, 1930–1940: A Historical and Statistical Profile." *Phylon 42*(2), 105–119.

McBrier, D., Wilson, G. (2004). "Going Down? Race and Downward Occupational Mobility for White-Collar Workers in the 1990s." *Work and Occupation 31*(3), 283–322.

McKay, C. (1940). *Harlem: Negro Metropolis.* New York: E. P. Dutton.

McLean, S. L., Schultz, D. A., Steger, M. B. (Eds.). (2002). *Social Capital: Critical Perspectives on Community and "Bowling Alone."* New York: New York University Press.

Merton, R. (1952). "Review of Warner and Lunt's 'The Social Life of a Modern Community.'" *Survey Graphic 31*, 438–439.

Michman, R. D., Mazze, E., Greco, A. (Eds.). (2003). *Lifestyle Marketing: Reaching the New American Consumer.* Westport, Conn.: Praeger.

Mills, C. (1942). "Review of Warner and Lunt's 'The Social Life of a Modern Community.'" *American Sociological Review 7*, 263–271.

Mills, C. W. (1957). *The Power Elite.* New York: Oxford University Press.

Moore, J. (1999). *Leading the Race: The Transformation of the Black Elite in the Nation's Capital, 1880–1920.* Charlottesville: University Press of Virginia.

Moreno, P. D. (1997). *From Direct Action to Affirmative Action: Fair Employment Law and Policy in America, 1933–1972.* Baton Rouge: Louisiana State University Press.

Morris, A. (1999). "A Retrospective on the Civil Rights Movement: Political and Intellectual Landmarks." *Annual Review of Sociology 25,* 517–539.

Morris, R. J. (2005). *Men, Women, and Property in England, 1780–1870: A Social and Economic History of Family Strategies Amongst the Leeds Middle Classes.* New York: Cambridge University Press.

Moss, J. (1979). "Brashler's Black Middle Class: A Rebuttal." *The Crisis 86*(7), 307–310.

————. (1991). "Hurling Oppression: Overcoming Anomie and Self Hatred." In B. Bowser (Ed.), *Black Male Adolescents: Parenting and Education in Community Context* (pp. 282–297). Lanham, Md.: University Press of America.

Moynihan, D. P. (1965). *The Negro Family, the Case for National Action.* Washington, D.C.: Superintendent of Documents, US Government Printing Office.

————. (1986). *Family and Nation.* San Diego, Calif.: Harcourt Brace Jovanovich.

Nakao, K., Treas, J. (1992). *The 1989 Socioeconomic Index of Occupations: Construction from the 1989 Occupational Prestige Scores.* Chicago: NORC.

Nam, C., Powers, M. (1965). "Variations in Socioeconomic Structure by Race, Residence and the Life Cycle." *American Sociological Review 30*(1), 97–104.

National Public Radio. (2006). "Black Student Enrollment at UCLA Plunges." Http://www.npr.org/templates/story/story.php?storyId=5563891.

Negus, K. (1999). "The Music Business and Rap: Between the Street and Executive Suite." *Cultural Studies 13*(3), 488–508.

Nelson, B. (2001). *Divided We Stand: American Workers and the Struggle for Black Equality*. Princeton, N.J.: Princeton University Press.

Newby, I. A. (1973). *Black Carolinians: A History of Blacks in South Carolina from 1895 to 1968*. Columbia: University of South Carolina Press.

Oakes, M., Rossi, P. (2003). "The Measurement of SES in Health Research: Current Practice and Steps Toward a New Approach." *Social Science and Medicine, 56*(4), 769–785.

Oliver, M., Shapiro, T. (1995). *Black Wealth/White Wealth: A New Perspective on Racial Inequality*. New York: Routledge.

Orr, A. J. (2003). "Black-White Differences in Achievement: The Importance of Wealth." *Sociology of Education, 76*(4), 281–305.

Oskerman, P. (2006). "The Wage Effects of High Performance Work Organizations in Manufacturing." *Industrial and Labor Relations Review 59*(2), 187.

Palm, F. C. (1936). *The Middle Classes: Then and Now*. New York: Macmillan.

Pattillo-McCoy, M. (1999). *Black Picket Fences: Privilege and Peril Among the Black Middle Class*. Chicago: University of Chicago Press.

Perse, E. M. (2001). *Media Effects and Society*. Mahwah, N.J.: L. Erlbaum Associates.

Pessen, E. (1973). *Riches, Class, Power Before the Civil War*. Lexington, Mass.: D. C. Heath.

———. (1974). *Three Centuries of Social Mobility in America*. Lexington, Mass.: D. C. Heath.

Phil, S. (2003). "African Americans and Mortgage Lending Discrimination." *Western Journal of Black Studies 27*(2), 65–80.

Phillips, K. (1993). *Boiling Point: Republicans, Democrats, and the Decline of Middle-Class Prosperity*. New York: Random House.

Piven, F., Cloward, R. (1993). *Regulating the Poor: The Functions of Public Welfare*. New York: Vintage Books.

Platt, J. (1998). *A History of Sociological Research Methods in America: 1920–1960*. New York: Cambridge University Press.

Plummer, B. G. (Ed.). (2003). *Window on Freedom: Race, Civil Rights, and Foreign Affairs, 1945–1988*. Chapel Hill: University of North Carolina Press.

Powdermaker, F. (1939). *After Freedom*. New York: Viking Press.

Putnam, R. D. (2000). *Bowling Alone: The Collapse and Revival of American Community*. New York: Simon and Schuster.

Rainwater, L., Yancey, W. (Eds.). (1967). *The Moynihan Report and the Politics of Controversy*. Cambridge, Mass.: MIT Press.

Reed, W. (2002). "The Middle Class Black Male." In J. Teele (Ed.), *E. Franklin Frazier and Black Bourgeoisie* (pp. 102–117). Columbia: University of Missouri Press.

Rich, A., Weaver, R. K. (2000). "Think Tanks in the U.S. Media." *Harvard International Journal of Press/Politics 5*(4), 81–102.

Richardson, H. C. (2001). *The Death of Reconstruction: Race, Labor, and Politics in the Post–Civil War North, 1865–1901*. Cambridge: Harvard University Press.

Robinson, J. P., Shaver, P., Wrightsman, L. (Eds.). (1999). *Measures of Political Attitudes*. San Diego, Calif.: Academic Press.

Rolston, B. (1993). "The Training Ground: Ireland, Conquest and Colonisation." *Race and Class 34*(4), 13–24.

Ross, S., Yinger, J. (2002). *The Color of Credit: Mortgage Discrimination, Research Methodology, and Fair-Lending Enforcement*. Cambridge, Mass.: MIT Press.

Royle, E. (1997). *Modern Britain: A Social History, 1750–1997*. New York: St. Martin's Press.

Savage, B. D. (2003). *Broadcasting Freedom: Radio, War and the Politics of Race 1938–1948*. Chapel Hill: University of North Carolina Press.

Sawires, J. N., Peacock, M. J. (2000). "Symbolic Racism and Voting Behavior on Proposition 209." *Journal of Applied Social Psychology 30*(10), 2092–2100.

Seeman, M. (1946). "Skin Color Values in Three All-Negro School Classes." *American Sociological Review 11*, 315–321.

"Separate and Unequal." (2000). *Forum for Applied Research and Public Policy 15*(3), 65.

Simon, J. (Ed.). (1995). *The State of Humanity*. Cambridge, Mass.: Blackwell.

Skocpol, T. (2000). *The Missing Middle: Working Families and the Future of American Social Policy*. New York: Norton.

Smith, S. (1995). *Sick and Tired of Being Sick and Tired*. Philadelphia: University of Pennsylvania Press.

Snowden, J. F. . (2002). "Writing About African Americans in American History." In B. Bowser and L. Kushnick (Eds.), *Against the Odds: Scholars Who Challenged Race in the Twentieth Century* (pp. 41–62). Amherst: University of Massachusetts Press.

Sowell, T. (1975). *Affirmative Action Reconsidered: Was It Necessary in Academia?* Washington, D.C.: American Enterprise Institute For Public Policy Research.

Stack, C. (1974). *All Our Kin*. New York: Basic Books.

Stampp, K. M. (1965). *The Era of Reconstruction, 1865–1877*. New York: Vintage Books.

Stouffer, S., et al. (1949a). *The American Soldier: Combat and Its Aftermath* (vol. 2). Princeton, N.J.: Princeton University Press.

———. (1949b). *The American Soldier: Experiments on Mass Communication* (vol. 3). Princeton, N.J.: Princeton University Press.

Strobel, F., Patterson, W. (1999). *The Coming Class War and How to Avoid It: Rebuilding the American Middle Class*. Armonk, N.Y.: M. E. Sharpe.

Sullivan, T., Warren, E., Westbrook, J. (2000). *The Fragile Middle Class: Americans in Debt*. New Haven, Conn.: Yale University Press.

Synnott, M. (1979). *The Half-opened Door: Discrimination and Admissions at Harvard, Yale, and Princeton, 1900–1970*. Westport, Conn.: Greenwood Press.

Tate, D., Gibson, G. (1980). "Socioeconomic Status and Black and White Intelligence Revisited." *Social Behavior and Personality: An International Journal 8*(2), 233–238.

Teele, J. (Ed.). (2002). *E. Franklin Frazier and Black Bourgeoisie.* Columbia: University of Missouri Press.

Tindall, G. B. (1966). *South Carolina Negroes, 1877–1900.* Baton Rouge: Louisiana State University Press.

Tolbert, C. J. (2003). "Revisiting the Racial Threat Hypothesis: White Voter Support for California's Proposition 209." *State Politics and Policy Quarterly 3*(2), 183–203.

Tucker, M. B., Mitchell-Kernan, C. (Eds.). (1995). *The Decline in Marriage Among African Americans: Causes, Consequences, and Policy Implications.* New York: Russell Sage Foundation.

US Census Bureau. (1979). *The Social and Economic Status of the Black Population in the United States, 1790–1978* (vol. Series P-23; no. 80). Washington, D.C.: US Government Printing Office.

———. (1990). *Statistical Abstract of the United States: 1990.* 110th ed. Washington, D.C.: US Government Printing Office.

———. (2001). *2001 Supplemental Survey Summary Tables,* PCT049B, PCT049A. http://factfinder.census.gov.

———. (2003a). *Survey of Income and Program Participation (SIPP), 2001 Panel, Wave 1 Core Microdata File.* Washington, D.C.: Census Bureau.

———. (2003b). "Table A-2. Percent of People 25 Years Old and Over Who Have Completed High School or College, by Race, Ethnic Origin and Sex: Selected Years 1940 to 2002." Population Division, US Department of Commerce, Washington, D.C.

———. (2004a). "Table A-1. School Enrollment of the Population 3 Years Old and Over, by Level and Control of School, Race, and Hispanic Origin: October 1955 to 2002." Population Division, US Department of Commerce, Washington, D.C.

———. (2004b). "Table A-3. Mean Earnings of Workers 18 Years and Over, by Educational Attainment, Race, Hispanic Origin, and Sex: 1975 to 2002." Population Division, US Department of Commerce, Washington, D.C.

———. (2006a). "Table H-1. Income Limits for Each Fifth and Top 5 Percent of Black and Non-Hispanic White Households: 1967–2005." Income Survey Branch, Housing and Household Economic Statistics Division, US Department of Commerce, Washington, D.C. www.census.gov/hhes/www/income/histinc/h01b.html.

———. (2006b). *Current Population Survey, Annual Social and Economic Supplements.* Poverty and Health Statistics Branch. www.census.gov.

US Department of Labor. (2004). *Monthly Labor Review.* http://www.bls.gov/opub/ted/2004/ aug/wk4/arto2.htm.

Valentine, C. (1968). *Culture and Poverty: Critique and Counter-Proposals.* Chicago: University of Chicago Press.

Verlindin, C. (1955). *L'esclavage Dans L'europe Médiévale.* Brugge, Belgium: De Tempel.

Wade, R. (1964). *Slavery in the Cities: The South, 1820–1860.* New York: Oxford University Press.

Wallerstein, I. (1974). *The Modern World-System.* New York: Academic Press.

———. (1980). *The Modern World-System II.* New York: Academic Press.

Warner, W., Meeker, M., Eells, K. (1960). *Social Class in America: A Manual of Procedure for the Measurement of Social Status.* New York: Harper.

Warner, W., Srole, L. (1945). *The Social Systems of American Ethnic Groups.* New Haven, Conn.: Yale University Press.

Warner, W. L., Lunt P. (1941). *The Social Life of a Modern Community.* New York: Yale University Press.

———. (1942). *The Social System of a Modern Community.* New Haven, Conn.: Yale University Press.

Warren, E., Tyagi, A. M. (2003). *The Two-income Trap: Why Middle-class Mothers and Fathers Are Going Broke.* New York: Basic Books.

Waters, M. C. (1999). *Black Identities: West Indian Immigrant Dreams and American Realities.* Cambridge: Harvard University Press.

Webb, G. (1998). *Dark Alliance: The CIA, the Contras, and the Crack Cocaine Explosion.* New York: Seven Stories Press.

Weber, M. (1947). *From Max Weber: Essays in Sociology.* New York: Oxford University Press.

Wechsler, H. (1977) *The Qualified Student: A History of Selective College Admission in America.* New York: Wiley.

"Whites Own Ten Times the Assets of Blacks." (1986). *Society* 24(1), 3–5.

Willhelm, S. (1971). *Who Needs the Negro?* Garden City, N.Y.: Doubleday.

Williams, C. (1971). *The Destruction of Black Civilizations: Great Issues of a Race from 4500 B.C. to 2000 A.D.* Dubuque, Iowa: Kendall/Hunt.

Wilson, R. J. (1968). *In Quest of Community: Social Philosophy in the United States, 1860–1920.* New York: Wiley.

Wilson, W. J. (1978). *The Declining Significance of Race: Blacks and Changing American Institutions.* Chicago: University of Chicago Press.

———. (1987). *The Truly Disadvantaged: The Inner City, the Underclass and Public Policy.* Chicago: University of Chicago Press.

Wood, P. (1995). "If Toads Could Speak": How the Myth of Race Took Hold and Flourished in the Minds of Europe's Renaissance Colonizers." In B. Bowser (Ed.), *Racism and Anti-Racism in World Perspective* (pp. 27–45). Thousand Oaks, Calif.: Sage Publications.

Woodson, C. G. (1918). *A Century of Negro Migration.* Washington, D.C.: Association for the Study of Negro Life and History.

Woodward, C. V. (1966). *The Strange Career of Jim Crow.* New York: Oxford University Press.

Wynn, N. A. (1971). "The Impact of the Second World War on the American Negro." *Journal of Contemporary History 6*, 42–53.

———. (1976). *The Afro-American and the Second World War.* New York: Holmes and Meier.

Yette, S. (1971). *The Choice: The Issue of Black Survival in America.* New York: Berkley Publishing.

Zieger, R. (1994). *American Workers, American Unions*. Baltimore, Md.: Johns Hopkins University Press.

Zunz, O., Schoppa, L., Hiwatari, N. (Eds.). (2002). *Social Contracts Under Stress: The Middle Class of America, Europe, and Japan at the Turn of the Century*. New York: Russell Sage Foundation.

Zweigenhaft, R., Domhoff, G. W. (1991). *Blacks in the White Establishment? A Study of Race and Class in America*. New Haven, Conn.: Yale University Press.

———. (1998). *Diversity in the Power Elite: Have Women and Minorities Reached the Top?* New Haven, Conn.: Yale University Press.

———. (2003). *Blacks in the White Elite: Will the Progress Continue?* Lanham, Md.: Rowman and Littlefield.

Index

A Better Chance (ABC), 143
Activism in the South (US), 59, 61
Affirmative action, 1, 3, 9, 73, 84, 88,
  101, 103–105, 108–109, 111, 122,
  148, 151; consensus in 1960s, 102;
  conservative opposition to, 108,
  145; during Black Reconstruction,
  39; impact on college admissions,
  106; premature loss of, 124; related
  to Executive Order No. 11246, 80.
  See also Johnson, Lyndon; replaced
  by diversity, 108; resulting from
  Civil Rights Acts (1964), 76; shift
  in criteria for, 107; waning support
  for, 106
Africa/African(s), 23–24, 28, 36, 74,
  77, 94, 138, 160; slaves, 27;
  renamed Negro or black, 35
African American/s. *See* Black America
African American Families course, 48
African American middle class. *See*
  Black middle class
Alabama, 32, 51; Montgomery, 74
Alpha Kappa Alpha: Mississippi
  Health Project, 59
American dream, 33, 81,146, 157
Anglo-American expectations, 67
Anglo conformity, 40–41
Anjelou, Maya, 143
Antipoverty bills, 79
Apartheid, 51, 78. *See also* Jim Crow
Appleton, Nathan, 34

Asia/Asian(s), 23, 74, 77–78, 121, 160

Baker, Frazier, 41
Baptists: First Baptists, 39; Second
  Baptists, 39
Black codes, 37
Black America: attainment in higher
  education, 115–116; black classes:
  absence of upper class, 141–143;
  black aristocracy, 91; black
  "bourgeoisie," 91; caste class
  during Jim Crow, 51;
  comprehensive model of, 63–64;
  divisions in classes, 56–58;
  expansion of underclass, 131–134,
  161; fragmentation of, 130; impact
  of drug trafficking on, 133; lower
  class, 93–94; moral-ethical
  dimension of, 59–60; secularization
  of, 128; working class: growth of
  working-class communities, 73;
  expansion post–World War II, 75,
  78; loss of jobs, 121; black/white
  college enrollment disparities,
  113–114; black/white disparity in
  earnings, 116–118, 121–122;
  expansion of underclass, 131–134;
  family decline and economic
  inequality, 155; family values, 60;
  growing power and militancy,
  79–80; hierarchy of former slaves,
  39; hip-hop as new social

About the Book

The widespread presence of successful African Americans in virtually all walks of life has led many in the United States to believe that the races are now on an equal footing—and that color blindness is the most appropriate way to deal with racial difference. In strong contrast, Benjamin Bowser argues that the seemingly comparable black and white middle classes, even though inextricably linked, in fact exist on entirely different economic planes.

Probing the subtle inner workings of contemporary class dynamics, Bowser demonstrates that belief in comparability is based not in reality, but in hopes, sentiment, and ideology. His focus on the structural barriers that underlie differences in black and white achievement makes it clear that the national racial dilemma has not been solved, but only transformed, and that issues of race and class are inseparable in the United States.

Benjamin P. Bowser is professor of sociology at California State University, East Bay. He is editor of *Racism and Anti-Racism in World Perspective* and coeditor (with Raymond Hunt) of *Impacts of Racism on White Americans*.